FOREWARNED

EXTRAORDINARY IRISH STORIES OF PREMONITIONS AND DREAMS

COLM KEANE

CAPEL ISLAND

First published in Ireland in 2011

by

CAPEL ISLAND PRESS
36 Raheen Park, Bray,
County Wicklow, Ireland

ISBN 978-0-9559133-3-4

Printed and bound by CPI Group (UK) Ltd, Croydon, CR0 4YY
Typesetting and cover design by Typeform Ltd

For Seán

COLM KEANE'S 21 books include the number one bestsellers *Going Home: Irish Stories From The Edge Of Death*, *Padre Pio: The Irish Connection* and *Nervous Breakdown*. He is a graduate of Trinity College, Dublin, and Georgetown University, Washington DC. As a broadcaster he won a Jacob's Award and a Glaxo Fellowship for European Science Writers. His nine chart bestsellers include *The Jobs Crisis*, *Death And Dying* and *The Stress File*.

CONTENTS

It's a poor sort of memory that only works backwards.

Through The Looking-Glass, Lewis Carroll

INTRODUCTION

This is a book about sensing and seeing the future. It features and explains the gut feelings we all have about forthcoming events. It also deals with dreams and forebodings. It is an Irish book to the extent that it contains stories from all four corners of Ireland. Its scope is international, however, in that it reflects experiences which are prevalent worldwide.

It is, in very many ways, a shocking book. Deaths foreseen, tragedies anticipated and disasters predicted are prominently featured. Catastrophes such as car smashes, plane crashes and even murders are foretold. Contributors describe the troubled and distressing feelings of anxiety and unease that often precede these adverse events.

Sometimes the news is good. Speckled throughout the three central chapters are stories that involve a lottery win, family reconciliations, an unexpected childbirth and a variety of other positive outcomes. Foresight, by ensuring that necessary steps are taken, has also enabled potential calamities to be given the widest of berths.

Interviewees in this book also describe dreams – those vivid, colourful, often confused series of fascinating and sometimes worrying images that come to us while asleep and occasionally when awake. Some are ominous and dark; others warm and comforting. All have heralded the future and warned of times ahead.

The origins of this book date back to my work on near-death experiences spanning the best part of three years and resulting in my first book on the topic, *Going Home*. It gradually came to my attention that some of those returning from near-death journeys found they had developed a keen ability to foresee happenings that had yet to take place. Their experiences were replicated in international studies.

By the time that my follow-up work on the near-death phenomenon – *The Distant Shore* – was being written, I had amassed a sufficiently large number of premonitions and predictive dreams to include a separate chapter in the book. After its publication more and more forewarnings – the vast majority unrelated to near-death experiences – came to light. Letters, texts, emails and phone calls poured in from all parts of the country. Following requests for further help from the local and national press, the core foundation of this current book – *Forewarned* – was laid.

Everyone wishes to sense the future. We attempt it every day. Whether it's the weather, our work, our family or our own mortality, we crave information that will warn us of the challenges we face. That's why we attend fortune-tellers, read our horoscopes and consult with psychics. It's also why we worry about the strange symbols and images contained in our dreams.

Few days pass without most of us having some sort of gut feeling about future occurrences. How often we say, 'I have a bad feeling that something will happen!' or 'It doesn't feel right!' or 'Something is going to go wrong!' Occasionally there is a mixture of factors in action – dreams, dark feelings, flash images and other bizarre elements – and this confusing overlap is reflected in at least some of the stories and chapters ahead.

Also, there may be doubts about the true causes of at least some of the forewarnings detailed in the following pages. We should never underestimate, for example, the possible role of chance or coincidence. Studies and other evidence, however, suggest that something more basic and primeval – something well beyond our scientific comprehension – is going on. You will likely agree that this is evident throughout the following narrative accounts.

To be forewarned is to be forearmed, we are so often told. Foreknowledge ensures that we are prepared, and preparation minimises doubt and uncertainty, boosting our self-assurance and confidence in the face of what's on its way. To know is to gain advantage, secure the upper hand, ensure we capitalise on the very best opportunities open to us as we progress. That, let's be fair, is where we would all like to be.

Perhaps some of us do it better than others. But maybe that's because only some of us are open to our predictive senses, receptive to them and willing to listen. Yet it would seem from the evidence that all of us have an ability to see ahead, to feel the future, to view pictures of time to come. It is this capacity within us that is described, analysed and assessed in the chapters ahead.

Colm Keane

FORETELLING THE FUTURE

When Ryan Magee, from Derry, won almost £6.5 million sterling on the EuroMillions lottery in February 2008, it would appear that more than luck was involved. He already knew the prize was his. His 'premonition', as he called it, was so strong that throughout the course of his work, on the day of the draw, he bought tickets in four different locations in Northern Ireland.

'In the week leading up to Friday's draw I was certain I would win,' Magee said in the immediate aftermath of securing his windfall. 'I just couldn't get it out of my head. So, on the day, while I was travelling on business, I bought tickets in Omagh, Strabane, Coleraine and Derry.'

Although Magee bought 11 tickets, it wasn't that he was a lottery fanatic. In fact, his multiple purchases were beyond the norm. 'My only regular flutter is three lines on the Saturday Lotto draw so my 11 tickets were out of the ordinary for me – I really did have that lucky feeling!'

The morning after hitting the jackpot, Magee realised his premonition had come true: 'The winning ticket was the last one of the 11 I checked, by which time the numbers were in my head so I knew straightaway that I'd won. But, despite my premonition, I still couldn't believe it. You hear people saying they have a feeling before they win it, and you don't believe them, but every time I saw a EuroMillions advert I had a feeling that it was going to be me.'

Call them what you wish – premonitions, gut feelings or presentiments – these forewarnings of future events are most common. At the very least, one in four Irish people will experience them, representing some one-and-a-half million people north and south of the border. This figure is likely to underestimate the true number as most people, at one time or another, report some sort of foreboding or presentiment. An even higher percentage – up to one-half the population – will have a telepathic experience.

Presuming that the forewarnings are not connected either to prior information or past experience, they are commonly referred to as premonitions – the word originating from the Latin *prae* meaning 'before' and *monēre* meaning 'to warn'. These gifts or talents are experienced by young and old. They also span all races and creeds. They are, however, more common among women than men.

The events they forewarn of normally occur within a short span of time. It is estimated that approximately one-half come to pass quickly, within two days, with the remainder taking place at a subsequent stage. Only one in five occurs in a time period in excess of a month. However, the outcomes can take much longer to materialise – up to eight-and-a-half years as reported in one study. The phenomenon is also reported worldwide.

Academy Award winner Shirley MacLaine – who appeared with Peter Sellers in the 1979 comedy-drama *Being There* – had a clear forewarning of her co-star's subsequent death. 'I was sitting in my living-room with some friends,' MacLaine explained. 'All of a sudden I stood up. I said, "Something is wrong with Peter Sellers." I was getting strange and frightening vibrations that seemed to be coming from him. At that moment the telephone rang. It was a reporter who told me Peter Sellers had just died.'

Actor Alec Guinness – renowned for his performances in *The Bridge On The River Kwai* and later in *Star Wars* – described a premonition he had of fellow-actor James Dean's death. After a chance meeting at the famous Hollywood hangout, the Villa Capri restaurant, Dean insisted on showing Guinness his new sports car. On seeing it, Guinness was immediately struck by a feeling of doom and said to Dean: 'If you get in that car, you will be found dead in it by this time next week.' Exactly a week later, on 30 September 1955, James Dean was killed when he crashed the car.

Another film star, Lindsay Wagner – famous for her T.V. role as the Bionic Woman, for which she received an Emmy Award in 1977 – was suddenly overwhelmed by a strange, nauseous feeling as she waited to board an American Airlines flight at O'Hare airport in Chicago. The feeling, which she couldn't explain, was so powerful that she cancelled her reservation. The DC-10 crashed shortly after takeoff, in May 1979, killing all the passengers and crew.

Princess Diana also had a forewarning, this time in 1978 and concerning her father. It took the form of an ominous feeling that he would collapse. Having told friends, she then put the premonition out of her mind. The following day, however, she was informed that Earl Spencer had indeed collapsed and soon learned that he had suffered a near-fatal haemorrhage. The after-effects would still be noticeable three years later when he walked his daughter down the aisle at London's St. Paul's Cathedral for her marriage to Prince Charles.

In effect, what we are concerned with in this book are two different phenomena beginning with the letter 'p'. The relevant words are 'premonition' and 'precognition'. It would be an error to become preoccupied with the precise definitions of each. Even though they have different connotations and meanings, the truth is that the dividing line between them is often blurred. A third phenomenon to be aware of, which also begins with the letter 'p', is 'prophecy'.

Essentially, premonitions involve a sense of foreboding about unknown future events. They often manifest themselves as vague feelings of unease. A person may be apprehensive, anxious, troubled, distressed or worried that something bad is about to occur, even though they don't know what it is. The person may say, 'I have a bad feeling that something is going to happen.'

Many report having 'gut feelings', 'butterflies in the tummy', 'sinking feelings in the stomach' or 'gut-wrenching sensations' of troubles ahead. Sometimes there is an onset of depression, the cause of which only becomes clear when the disaster occurs. It is only then – after the event – that people say, 'I knew it was coming. I knew something was going to take place.'

Precognition, on the other hand, has less to do with a general feeling and more to do with an actual picture – often visualised while dreaming – of what lies ahead, such as an accident, car crash or death. For example, Sitting Bull foresaw in a vision that he would die at the hands of a member of his tribe dressed as a policeman, with one shot entering his head and another entering his side. Uncannily, in December 1890, it was a Sioux tribesman in police employment who killed him in exactly the manner he had predicted.

Prophecy is similar to precognition in that it also involves an image about a future event. The difference, however, is that prophecies are normally divinely inspired and usually concern big events that affect races of people or countries. Prophecies most often have their roots in ancient times and are especially, although not exclusively, concerned with religions. As such, they lie outside the scope of this book.

People often lump these different categories together and – incorrectly, it might be pointed out – refer to them all as premonitions. They may, for example, describe a clear-cut dream image as a premonition when it should really be referred to as precognition. In reality, however, people's experiences may not be exclusively confined to any single category – they may, instead, involve a mixture of more than one. This slightly confusing overlap will be evident in the main chapters of this book, but it's of no real importance or consequence.

Irrespective of the categories they belong to, examples of ominous forewarnings are littered throughout Irish history and mythology. One story involves the tragic pre-Christian heroine Deirdre, who is best known as 'Deirdre of the Sorrows'. Shortly before her birth, it was foreseen that she would be a beautiful woman and would bring bloodshed and strife to Ulster. As recounted in her saga, her beauty resulted in considerable conflict and death.

Deirdre had experiences of her own, including accurately identifying the man she would marry. She later foresaw that tragedy would ensue if she and her lover, who had eloped to Scotland, returned to Ulster. During their passage home by sea, she spotted what she perceived to be an inauspicious blood-red cloud. That sighting did indeed prove to be prophetic as their lives soon came to a wretched end.

The final battle involving Cú Chulainn is also laden with predictions and omens pertaining to his death. The bloodshed to come is foretold by the infamous Morrigan, or 'phantom queen', who often revealed herself as a crow. On the day of battle, as Cú Chulainn flung on his gown, his brooch fell and pierced his foot. Shortly afterwards, as he tried to harness his horse, it turned from him three times. These incidents were regarded as omens of the mythical hero's forthcoming demise.

Among many twentieth-century Irish examples is a story recounted by actor and co-founder of Dublin's Gate Theatre, Micheál Mac Liammóir. He described how, while walking one morning in Dublin's St. Stephen's Green, in the mid-1930s, he bumped into a wealthy, eccentric Irish-American who was known to him. 'You're going to America,' she exclaimed out of nowhere. 'Oh yes, you're going to America, because it has all been revealed to me.' 'What makes you so certain I'm going to America?' Mac Liammóir asked. 'Well, aren't you?' she responded.

The conversation was especially strange because, at the time, Mac Liammóir was carrying in his pocket a cable from the American actor Orson Welles, which had arrived that very morning, requesting both himself and his partner and colleague Hilton Edwards to join Welles in a summer season in Illinois. 'Here I was in Stephen's Green with Orson's cable burning me,' the actor concluded, 'and Vivian with her demented psychic smile prophesying the inevitable with the confidence of the Delphic oracle.'

Further strange forewarnings were associated with the Abbey actress Molly Allgood, who shortly after the turn of the twentieth century became the fiancée of playwright John Millington Synge. During a tour of England, Allgood – who was better known by her stage name Máire O'Neill – reported that while she and Synge were seated in a tea shop, the flesh appeared to peel away from Synge's face to reveal his skull. Later, as Synge was awaiting an operation, she had a dream of him being lowered in his coffin into a grave. Synge died soon after, on 24 March 1909, from cancer.

So far, I have largely ignored the most important mechanism through which so many forewarnings emerge – dreams. Predictive dreams, in the main, are highly realistic, with the information or images being presented in a straightforward manner and closely replicating the later event. A smaller number of dream images are represented symbolically or in an obscure way, making them harder to recognise or interpret.

Dreams, of course, are not confined to our sleep. There are also daydreams – those dream-like mental images or fanciful thoughts that surface in our minds while awake. These 'waking thoughts' or 'waking images' are often happy and pleasant but not always – they can be distasteful and unsavoury. Just like sleeping dreams, they can forewarn us of future happenings ranging from the commonplace to major events.

Although studied throughout history, the role of dreams in predicting the future is still not fully understood. The evidence is confusing. For a start, not all dreams are predictive with many having nothing to do with future events. It would also appear that some people, especially women, experience predictive dreams more than others. Perhaps, it is suggested, those who have 'thinner boundaries' are more sensitive and receptive to information from beyond the five physical senses – which is exactly the place from which our dreams emerge.

Documents detailing the earliest dream insights and revelations were discovered in Egypt and date to over 1,000 years before Christ. Ancient Egyptian papyrus scripts describe how dreams were believed to contain communications from the gods. The Egyptians even had a god of dreams, named Serapis. People would prepare themselves before going to temples where they would await dream communications. What was revealed to them would be interpreted later on by learned men.

The Romans had a much more intense preoccupation with dreams and other presentiments. Before crossing the Rubicon and marching on Rome, Caesar dreamt that he engaged in an incestuous act with his mother. This was interpreted as meaning that 'Mother Rome' would be happy to welcome him and not resist. His conquest of Rome was successful. Much later, Calpurnia, Caesar's wife, foresaw her husband's murder and pleaded with him not to go to the Senate on the day he was killed.

It is further reported that, on his way to the Senate, Caesar met with a seer who had earlier predicted that he would be harmed not later than the Ides of March. 'The Ides of March have come,' Caesar admonished the seer. 'They have come but they are not gone,' the seer responded. Caesar was assassinated later that day, the Ides of March 44 B.C.

The Old Testament, not surprisingly, also contains some remarkable warnings revealed through dreams. Perhaps the best known involves the Pharaoh – the title for the ancient Egyptian king – who dreamt that while standing by the Nile, out of the river came seven cows, sleek and fat. They were followed by another seven cows, gaunt and ugly.

The latter ate up the former, after which the Pharaoh woke up. His dreams were interpreted by Joseph, one of the great Old Testament figures, as a sign that seven years of abundance would be followed by seven years of famine. Historical research indicates that something not dissimilar happened.

What may cause premonitions and precognition will be examined later on in this book. In the meantime, we may speculate that they are the direct product of some sort of extraordinary natural ability to see into the future. Perhaps all of us have inherited this instinct since primitive times. Alternatively, out of necessity, we may have developed this capacity in our struggle to survive.

What is most mysterious, though, is why certain people experience forewarnings more than others – and some not at all. Perhaps particular types of people are more open to psychic suggestion. With scientific advancements, maybe less of us rely on our senses and instincts. Yet it is possible that all of us, underneath, possess an ingrained, innate ability, lodged somewhere in the subconscious, which is ready to prompt us to spring into action.

Also of interest is the obvious and clear-cut association between dark, tragic or catastrophic events and forewarnings. Numerous research studies have identified this link. Why is it that deaths of close relatives or friends are such a common theme, as are disasters and other calamities? Why is it, to the contrary, that calm and happy events so seldom feature? Do tragic events somehow cast dark shadows before them?

That intense events such as deaths and catastrophes are so prevalent and widely reported is perhaps not surprising. The happenings are not only dramatic but they also involve high levels of tension and anxiety and, as such, are more likely to force their way through to our minds and our senses. They are, from that point of view, more likely to be recorded and recalled. In sharp contrast, trivial events tend to be ignored.

One of the most devastating and tragic events in modern history must surely be the catastrophe now known as 9/11. On that day – Tuesday, 11 September 2001 – some 3,000 people lost their lives after four hijacked planes were crashed into the World Trade Center, the Pentagon and a field in Pennsylvania. Many premonitions and precognitions were reported around the event – some in advance of the tragedy and told to friends, relatives or work colleagues; more surfacing after the event had taken place.

One premonition involved Lawrence Boisseau, a 36-year-old fire safety director who worked at the World Trade Center. A short time before the disaster, Boisseau had a dream that the towers were crashing down around him. A few days later, his wife dreamt that the Manhattan streets were covered in debris. Just two days before the tragedy, the couple spoke about death. 'If the time comes, if you need somebody to take care of you, I don't mind,' he told his wife. Despite the forewarnings, Boisseau went to work on 9/11 and perished.

Eamon J. McEneaney, who was a senior vice-president at the brokerage firm Cantor Fitzgerald, also travelled to his office at the World Trade Center on that horrific September day. He, too, had premonitions of the disaster ahead. Years beforehand, he informed his family that he was destined to die around the turn of the century – the year he specified being 2001. Just days prior to the catastrophe, he discussed with his brother possible exit routes from the towers in the event of terrorist attacks. He also informed his wife that he was ready for death. McEneaney died in the tragedy.

Another tragic 9/11 victim was Tom Burnett, who was a passenger aboard United Airlines flight 93, which crashed in Pennsylvania. Burnett had long believed he would die young and had discussed the issue with his wife. He also believed that his death would in some way be connected with the White House. His wife, Deena, had a feeling that her husband wouldn't live long enough to raise the couple's children. Tom Burnett died when the now-infamous flight 93 was brought down by hijackers on what is believed to have been an attempt to fly it into the White House.

The actress Alicia Silverstone, who is best known for her performances in *Clueless* and as Batgirl in *Batman & Robin*, also had a premonition on the morning of 9/11. She woke up feeling that a family member was dead. Although unaware of the tragedy, at that stage, it later transpired that her cousin Lisa Trerotola – who worked as a secretary for the New York Port Authority – had been killed in the World Trade Center attacks. 'In my gut, I knew we'd suffered a loss in the family,' the actress said later.

Continuing with 9/11, the actor Michael Caine recently explained how he once dreamed up the plot for a novel involving terrorists crashing a plane into a skyscraper. He had begun writing his book when the attack on the World Trade Center took place in 2001. 'I had this plot where terrorists fly a plane into a London skyscraper,' he said. 'Then they did it in real life. I was stunned by that, so I stopped writing.'

Forewarnings were also reported prior to another dark and depressing event – the disaster which took place in the Welsh mining village of Aberfan in 1966. On Friday, 21 October, 116 children and 28 adults died when a river of coal waste and boulders slid down from a man-made mountain and crashed into a school. Most of the schoolchildren who died were aged between seven and ten.

Although many claimed *following* the event to have had forebodings of the disaster, one story *predated* the tragedy and had the ring of cast-iron truth. The story concerned ten-year-old Eryl Mai Jones, who earlier that week had said to her mother, 'I'm not afraid to die. I shall be with Peter and June.'

The day before the catastrophe, she also spoke of a dream. 'I dreamt I went to school and there was no school there,' she said. 'Something black had come down all over it.' Eryl Mai Jones died on that unfortunate day in 1966 and was later buried alongside her friends Peter and June.

Further forebodings were associated with the Air France Concorde crash in Paris in 2000, which killed all on board. Following the tragedy, one of the airline's Concorde staff – a pilot – claimed that they had felt trouble coming. A 'morbid expectation of an accident' had gripped the 36-strong team of pilots, co-pilots and engineers in the months leading up to the disaster, the crew member said. 'I had this sense that we were going to bump into the scenery,' he remarked. 'It was as if I was waiting for something to happen.'

It is worth noting how dark forewarnings, similar to those just recounted, can sometimes enable people who receive them to avoid tragedies ahead. This theme was examined in the Stargate Project undertaken by the US government from the 1970s – 1990s. The project examined how various human psychic phenomena might be of help to the military and the CIA. Among the areas investigated were 'remote viewing' – the ability to view things from afar by paranormal means – and the ability to sense or see the future.

Stargate researchers were particularly impressed by the behaviour patterns and psychic skills of those they referred to as 'lucky soldiers' – namely, military personnel who exhibited extraordinary extrasensory skills which allowed them to forecast ahead and survive battles. It quickly became clear that certain soldiers used feelings and thoughts – not to mention glimpses of the future – to defy impossible odds.

This apparent ability to circumvent future dark moments would also appear to extend well beyond the battlefields of wartime. It has been noted, for example, how a significant number of people avoid booking themselves onto trains, boats or planes that crash. Some people find innumerable excuses not to book in the first place. Others appear to intuitively cancel at the last moment.

That this is the case has been amply demonstrated in a fascinating investigation undertaken by American researcher William Cox back in the mid-1950s. Using data for 28 train crashes occurring from 1950 – 1955, Cox set out to compare occupancy rates in trains that crashed with those that arrived safely. To achieve this, he compared the rate on the day of each crash with rates for other days during the preceding week and on equivalent days in earlier weeks.

The results were remarkable. In all cases, fewer people travelled on the trains that crashed than on similar trains that didn't crash. In one case alone, only nine passengers travelled on a train that crashed compared to a more typical complement numbering into the low 60s. The odds of Cox's conclusions happening by chance – estimated at 1 in 100 – were small. For some strange reason, on days when trains were facing collisions an unusually high number of people stayed at home or found other ways to travel.

Occupancy rates – the percentages of seats filled – have similarly been shown to be lower on doomed aircraft. Only 22 per cent of seats were occupied on the Boeing 757 that crashed into the Pentagon on 9/11. The occupancy rates for the planes that smashed into the North and South Towers of the World Trade Center were a mere 26 per cent and 19 per cent respectively. The average occupancy rate for all four tragic planes, that day, was an unusually low 21 per cent.

We may ask: did potential passengers visualise trouble ahead? Perhaps they developed a gut feeling that something was wrong? Maybe some subconscious trigger warned them to postpone their journeys or not travel at all? Or possibly, of course, the apparent cause-and-effect was the result of some sort of meaningless coincidence, chance aberration or false correlation. The occupancy rates, however, appear to be so abnormally low that this latter proposition is unlikely.

This reluctance to travel on doomed planes has resulted in many passengers cheating death. Stefan van Oss – who was scheduled to travel on the Air France flight that crashed on 1 June 2009 – was one of those fortunate passengers. His flight, which was travelling from Rio de Janeiro to Paris, plunged into the Atlantic Ocean killing all 228 passengers and crew. Van Oss, however, wasn't on board having cancelled his journey after a friend warned him of danger.

Two other passengers, Johanna Ganthaler and her husband Kurt, arrived late for that same flight and were unable to board. The couple booked themselves on a later flight, thus avoiding the tragedy. The Ganthalers' luck didn't last long, however, as their car crashed into an oncoming truck en route from the flight to their residence in Italy's Bolzano-Bozen province. Johanna died in the crash; her husband was seriously injured.

Low occupancy rates also pertained in the case of the doomed *Titanic*. The White Star Line managed to fill only slightly more than 50 per cent of the available passenger accommodation for its maiden voyage, which came to a disastrous end on the night of 14 – 15 April 1912. At least 55 people – about four per cent of the total expected aboard – had a change of mind and cancelled at short notice.

The list included John Pierpont Morgan, who was ultimate owner of the White Star Line, and his former business partner Robert Bacon, who was the departing American Ambassador to France. Others included the steel magnate Henry C. Frick and the railway and shipping mogul George W. Vanderbilt. Professor Ian Stevenson, of the University of Virginia, documented 19 experiences relating to the *Titanic* which involved forewarnings consisting mostly of general hunches or dreams.

One anecdote pertaining to the *Titanic* concerned Patrick O'Keefe, a 21-year-old labourer from Waterford. He was returning to America following a holiday in Ireland. While asleep in lodgings at Cobh (then known as Queenstown) on the night before his departure, he had a foreboding of disaster ahead. 'I dreamt myself she was going down before I left Queenstown,' he wrote to his father in a letter shortly after his rescue, 'and I thought to sell my passage note for seven pounds.' O'Keefe survived by jumping from the sinking ship and swimming to a nearby lifeboat.

Less fortunate was Chief Officer Henry Wilde, who had reluctantly joined the crew. In a letter posted during the ship's stopover at Cobh, he wrote to his sister: 'I still don't like this ship ...... I have a queer feeling about it.' Despite his reservations, Wilde sailed to his death on the liner. One of the ship's firemen, John Coffey, from Cobh, was luckier – he hid himself in one of the postbags and smuggled himself ashore before the liner set sail following its brief stopover in County Cork.

Undoubtedly the most perplexing *Titanic* forewarning – or strange coincidence, if it should be such – involved the novel *Futility*, which was published 14 years before the ship sank. Written by the American amateur mystic Morgan Robertson, the similarity between the contents of his book and the actual details pertaining to the *Titanic* were startling.

Robertson's fictional ship, ominously called the *Titan*, had virtually the same top speed, capacity, length, number of lifeboats, number of passengers, number of propellers and displacement as the *Titanic*. The two ships sailed under the British flag. Both sailed in April – and both hit an iceberg and sank!

Premonitions and precognition are also closely associated with the violence and emotions of another intense activity – warfare. In some cases, a soldier on the battlefront foresees his own death. In other cases, family and friends at home anticipate the pending tragedy. Sometimes the soldier dies. Other times intervention saves him. All of these cases involve fraught environments, filled with stress and strain, where tension is high and pressure often unbearable.

The well-known investigator of psychic phenomena, Dr. Hereward Carrington, has examined this theme in a brilliant and comprehensive study published in 1918. He concluded: 'Men and women, under certain stresses of the mind or of the emotions, or in certain peculiar or ill-understood states, which often seem to appear quite spontaneously – do in fact partly and dimly vision the future.'

In America, Custer's last stand at the Little Bighorn produced many uncanny premonitions. One cavalryman, Captain Myles Keogh, who came from County Carlow, asked a fellow officer shortly before the battle for help in drawing up his will. He also took out an insurance policy and, while appearing unusually gloomy, he wrote that the month of June 'has never passed since I left home without something very unpleasant occurring to me.' He was killed at the Little Bighorn.

One of Custer's scouts, 'Lonesome' Charley Reynolds, had similar bad feelings about the expedition that led to the massacre. He was refused permission by his commanding officer to be released from service, which he requested on two occasions, and died in the fray. Even Custer's wife, Elizabeth, was overcome by a feeling of doom and sensed the calamity to come.

On the Indian side, Sioux chief Sitting Bull informed his tribe of visions which included images of white men dying on Sioux land in their hundreds, as if 'fallen from the sky.' He also foresaw that the Sioux warriors would win the battle. Both premonitions came true when Custer's Seventh Cavalry was wiped out in the slaughter which took place from 25 – 26 June 1876.

Some other wartime premonitions or precognition – involving World War I – were chronicled by Dr. Hereward Carrington, who was referred to earlier. Among the cases he recorded was the story of a lieutenant who had a clear vision of his forthcoming death. 'I shall be wounded four times, and my fourth wound will kill me,' the lieutenant told friends.

Events unfolded exactly as he predicted. On three different occasions he was wounded and came home on sick leave. At the end of his third spell of leave he told his family before returning to the front, 'You will not see me again.' He died soon after, in Rouen, from wounds inflicted to his skull.

In another story, also recorded by Carrington, a woman from London by the name of Mrs. Parker recalled a dream she had on 4 February 1916. In it, she saw a coffin being carried into her home by four soldiers and set down inside the front door on two chairs. A man in plain clothes stood nearby, looking grave. He opened the coffin lid to allow her to see inside. 'She gave a scream of agony and terror as in the cold, waxen, lifeless features she recognised the face of her son,' the author wrote.

The following morning, Mrs. Parker received word that her son was seriously ill. Three days later, he died. Then, exactly as she foresaw, the coffin containing the corpse was carried into her house by four soldiers and set down on two chairs in the hall. A man in plain clothes, who turned out to be an undertaker, and who was positioned nearby, stepped forward to open the lid of the coffin so that she might have a last look. Mrs. Parker's dream had come to fruition in uncanny detail.

I have, up to now, neglected to mention the concept of 'intuition', which also needs to be considered in the context of the theme of this book. Intuition refers to that capacity within us to comprehend in the mind without resorting to any rational process. It is a fascinating instinct, valuable, inexplicable and located well beyond the realms of conscious thought.

Most importantly, intuition is real, perhaps based on knowledge and observation and certainly not a by-product of chance or coincidence. Our minds cannot influence it. Children use it extensively. So do women, who have been shown to reveal greater intuitive skills than men. They possess a greater sense of 'knowing'.

This subconscious sensation of reality enables and allows us to instantaneously resolve problems without having to contemplate all the factors involved. Once we are introduced to new people, it allows us to decide who to like or avoid. It may help us to steer clear of accidents or other calamities. It may also inspire us to great discoveries or insights.

The physicist and Nobel Prize winner Albert Einstein was aware of its value in securing the great advances of mankind. 'The intellect has little to do on the road to discovery,' he remarked. 'There comes a leap in consciousness, call it intuition or what you will, and the solution comes to you and you don't know how or why.'

The pivotal importance of intuition in business decision-making has been particularly noted. For example, Ray Kroc used his intuitive powers when buying the small family hamburger business in southern California that he eventually developed into the worldwide McDonalds chain. 'It's my intuition that pushed me to purchase,' he said. Sam Walton, who founded Walmart, also relied on his intuitive powers when setting up his low-cost retail chain.

Other tycoons went even further by using the intuitive or predictive skills of experts when searching for the perfect deal. The oil magnate H. L. Hunt, who was one of the richest men in America by the time of his death in 1974, went so far as to employ the help of a psychic when selecting oil properties. The financier and banker J. P. Morgan used fortune-tellers. Many studies show that these examples are far from isolated.

Although sometimes said to have supernormal origins, these intuitive business abilities are more likely to be the by-product of past experience and knowledge built up over time. By way of example, we might expect senior business executives, who have progressed through many long years of decision-making, to have a sense of how future events might evolve. Studies examining this theme paint an intriguing picture.

Perhaps the most fascinating study was undertaken back in the 1970s by American researchers Douglas Dean and John Mihalasky, from the Newark College of Engineering. They carried out a series of experiments analysing the predictive powers of chief executive officers of American corporations. The conclusions were remarkable.

Some 80 per cent of the business leaders who had doubled or nearly doubled their profits over a five-year period had the best predictive powers. The connection was so strong that the research team was able to scrutinise financial reports and predict how any particular executive would perform in their experiments.

A further study was undertaken by Corvinus University of Budapest, in Hungary. This study similarly concluded that top managers used both rational and intuitive skills in strategic decision-making. The study additionally emphasised the importance attributed by top management to non-rational skills. 'They rely heavily on intuition,' the researchers concluded regarding the executives surveyed.

The Corvinus study also compared results for conventional business executives and entrepreneurs. Executives generally followed safer business strategies and outperformed their entrepreneurial counterparts in terms of classic skills such as organising and analysing. Entrepreneurs, on the other hand, made more use of intuitive skills and, as a result, were more adept at risk-taking.

The role of animal intuition has also been noted. Dogs exhibit an intuitive ability enabling them to predict when their owners are about to return home. Wild animals, such as elephants, monkeys and birds, commonly flee territories where earthquakes, tsunamis or volcanoes are about to occur. Many leave as early as a week before the disaster. Pet dogs were reported to have refused their daily walks on the beach prior to the 2004 Indian Ocean tsunami, which killed some one-quarter of a million people.

Many reasons have been put forward as to why animals behave in this way. Perhaps, in the case of pets, they have developed emotional bonds with their owners that border on the telepathic. Maybe all animals have a more intense connection with their environments than humans, which allows them a much greater sensitivity to vibrations and atmospheric changes. To put this in a different way, it may be that animals have more finely-tuned 'automatic radars' – keener senses that have been dulled in humans over time – which permit them to foretell dangers ahead.

Before ending this chapter, it is also important to mention one final factor that may lead us to draw spurious conclusions about apparent connections between unconnected events. The factor in question is 'coincidence'. To put it quite simply, a coincidence is said to have arisen when two or more happenings occur by chance. There is no other meaningful connection between the occurrences. No other relationship is involved.

Coincidence is a remarkable phenomenon. The American novelist Anne Parrish, back in the 1920s, travelled to Paris with her husband. While there, she was browsing in a bookshop when she came across a well-worn copy of *Jack Frost And Other Stories*, which was a book she had loved as a child. Her husband, on opening the book, was shocked to read the inscription inside, 'Anne Parrish, 209 N. Weber Street, Colorado Springs, Colorado.'

An equally remarkable story, from Ireland, is related by

the twentieth-century author Arthur Koestler. Following the publication of his book *The Roots Of Coincidence* in 1972, he was bombarded with letters from all over the world. One letter came from Anthony Clancy of Dublin, who described how he was born on the seventh day of the seventh month of the seventh year of the century. The day he was born was the seventh day of the week.

Clancy went on to explain how he was the seventh child of a seventh child and had seven brothers. His first name, Anthony, contained seven letters. He also described how he once bet on a horse on his twenty-seventh birthday. The horse he selected was the seventh numbered horse in the seventh race, named Seventh Heaven. He bet seven shillings at odds of seven to one. The horse, unfortunately, came seventh!

This story – whether true or contrived – illustrates the vital importance of considering either chance or coincidence when assessing apparent connections between events. Statistically, coincidences do happen and indeed are inevitable. Some people, however, urge caution. There are no coincidences, they claim. Instead, everything, no matter how trivial, has a cause or a connection, whether seen or unseen, recognised or unrecognisable.

One woman who contacted me in the course of my own research – Mary, from County Down – took up this theme. She described how, in 2001, she and her family were on holidays in Spain. They stayed in apartments located near the beach but which also possessed an enclosed swimming-pool in a locked courtyard. Each guest held a key to the courtyard, which Mary's apartment overlooked.

One day, on returning from the beach, she placed her key to the courtyard on the table inside her apartment door. This action was unusual for her to take. Soon afterwards, from her balcony, having been alerted by her child, she spotted a young girl lying face down in the pool. 'I grabbed the keys and ran down the stairs and opened the courtyard door,' Mary explained. 'The girl was face down, unconscious and had drowned. I gave the child CPR and, when the ambulance came, she had a pulse.

'It was strange how I had consciously put the keys on the hall table. It was strange how I was on the balcony just at the right time. It was strange how we spotted the child. I believe I was meant to be in that place at that time. I don't believe in chance or coincidence. Instead, I believe our paths were meant to cross.'

While allowing for the possible involvement of intuition and chance, which we have just addressed, it would be foolish to dismiss the role of premonitions and precognition in sensing and seeing the future. There is compelling scientific evidence to suggest that the phenomena are real and do happen. The final chapter in this book will examine this evidence.

In addition, the chapters containing real-life Irish stories will demonstrate how forthcoming events are frequently foretold with astonishing accuracy. But, of course, it is not just in Ireland that instances of these otherwise inexplicable forewarnings are to be found – they are prevalent worldwide.

One of the most extraordinary instances took place in 1950 in the tiny town of Beatrice, Nebraska, USA. The town, which is located south of Lincoln, on the Big Blue River, was the setting on 1 March of that year for a truly remarkable event. The happening occurred at the West Side Baptist Church, where 15 choir members were due to attend practice at 7.20 p.m.

All 15 choir members were uncommonly late. The minister, along with his wife and daughter, missed the agreed time because the minister's wife delayed to iron a dress for their daughter. One girl struggled to finish her homework. Another girl waited to hear the end of a radio programme, causing her friend to be late as well. Yet another choir member, who lived just across the street, delayed to the last minute because of the cold weather.

The pianist, who had planned to arrive 30 minutes early, fell asleep after dinner with the result that she and her mother were also behind time. One more choir member had to visit her mother's house to deal with a minor matter. Others were late because of car trouble or, in one case, because the choir member was composing a letter. In all, there were ten separate and unconnected reasons why, of the 15 choir members, no one was there.

At exactly 7.25 p.m. – with the church still empty – a massive explosion tore apart the West Side Baptist Church in the town of Beatrice. The blast occurred in the boiler room, right underneath the choir loft. The walls collapsed outwards and the roof fell downwards. The church steeple fell onto the street. The town's lights went out, windows were shattered and a nearby radio station was taken off the air. A gas explosion, perhaps linked to the boiler furnace, was identified as the likely cause.

A feature in *Life* magazine, less than four weeks later, quoted some choir members as saying that the event was 'an act of God.' Their belief was understandable as this, after all, was the first time in the choir's history that everyone was late as a unit. Was it chance, maybe a one-in-a-million occurrence? Or perhaps it was something more? 'I kept putting off going out the door,' Joyce Black, who lived just across the street, explained. 'At last, I couldn't put it off any longer and when I opened up the door our church disintegrated.'

It is stories such as these, along with the scientific evidence, that has convinced esteemed figures from the world of science that the future can indeed be seen. 'I believe that we can sense the future,' concludes Professor Brian Josephson, who won a Nobel Prize in 1973 for his work on superconductivity. 'We just haven't yet established the mechanism allowing it to happen.'

His viewpoint is echoed by the well-known Dutch parapsychologist Professor Dick Bierman. 'We're satisfied that people can sense the future before it happens,' he concludes. 'We'd now like to move on and see what kind of person is particularly good at it.' This goal of identifying the many different types of people who possess these remarkable skills, and recording their narratives, is a worthwhile one. It is a challenge taken up in the following pages, where the real-life stories of Irish people who have glimpsed or sensed the future are presented.

STRANGE PREMONITIONS

When the eminent fashion designer Lady Lucy Duff Gordon booked her berth on the ill-fated *Titanic*, she had a feeling that something was wrong. 'Of all things,' the booking agent assured her, 'I should imagine you could not possibly feel nervous on the *Titanic*. Why, the boat is absolutely unsinkable.'

Whether Duff Gordon was temporarily reassured by the agent or just under pressure to travel isn't known. Either way, this remarkable woman – who was the first British designer of international renown and the originator of the fashion show – boarded the liner and sailed for New York.

Lady Duff Gordon would later describe how, throughout the four-day journey before the ship sank, she was overcome by a 'feeling of acute fear.' Despite being pampered as a first-class passenger – and looked after by an Irish stewardess – the ominous sensation persisted.

'Nothing could persuade me to completely undress at night, and my warm coat and wrap lay always ready at hand,' she later explained. 'My little jewel case, with a few of my most treasured possessions, was placed on a convenient table within my reach.'

Four days into its journey, late on the night of 14 April 1912, the infamous *Titanic* struck an iceberg and two hours and forty minutes later it sank. Among the lucky survivors were Lady Lucy Duff Gordon and her husband Sir Cosmo Duff Gordon who had accompanied her on the trip.

Despite her good fortune, she never forgot that pre-tragedy feeling of doom. 'Though I have crossed the Atlantic many times both before and since I have never had it on any other occasion,' she later wrote. 'Something warned me, some deep instinct, that all was not well.'

It is precisely that sensation of unease or gut feeling that characterises premonitions and makes them so frightening. Those who experience them sense that something is about to happen but they can't identify what it is. The future event remains unknown. The tense, uneasy feeling persists until the happening occurs and, once it does, relief normally follows.

Premonitions, in that sense, differ considerably from the predictive dreams, or precognition, which are discussed in the next chapter. In the case of precognition an image is perceived of a future event which then comes to pass. The image is central. In the case of premonitions, by way of contrast, the sensation is the key.

In both these cases – premonitions and predictive dreams – experiences can happen more than once. People with multiple stories to tell are commonplace. You need look no further than to the post-*Titanic* experience of Lady Duff Gordon, who lived until the ripe age of 71, to establish the case.

Three years after her initial near-tragedy, Duff Gordon was booked to sail on the *Lusitania*, which was torpedoed and sunk off the Old Head of Kinsale, County Cork. Some 1,200 people died. But Duff Gordon wasn't on board. Officially, at least, she had cancelled her trip due to illness. Sometimes, as we shall see in the stories ahead, the truth can be stranger than fiction.

BEVERLEY, FROM COUNTY DOWN, had a premonition, in the mid-2000s, that she was about to be involved in a car crash.

I woke up one morning, at about half-six, to go to work. It was around mid-February to late February. I remember it was a sunny day, with very good weather. From the moment I put my feet on the floor, I had a phrase in my head. It just popped into it from nowhere. It said, 'Head-on collision!'

From the minute I stood on the floor until I went into the shower, the phrase stayed with me. I worked, at the time, a fairly long distance away and I used to drive there. When I got into the car the phrase was there again. I think I had it one more time on the way to work.

The phrase came to me on a number of occasions during the day. It happened about a half-a-dozen times, especially around lunchtime. It was always the exact same, 'Head-on collision!' It didn't really intrude but it was there. It was like a shadow overhanging me.

I felt that the phrase was very curious. I kept wondering, 'What's this about?' Nothing like this had ever happened to me before. It was like something was being flagged. It made me feel, 'I'd better beware. I'd better be extra alert today.' I sort of felt, 'Today is a good day for an accident,' although I don't know why I felt that.

Maybe it was because I was doing the same drive a lot that I wondered, 'You've done this journey so many times and statistically you might have an accident today.' There were also lots of crazy drivers on those country roads. However, as the morning went on, although I still hadn't driven home, the feeling eased and I thought, 'There's nothing to be afraid of.'

That day I had to come home by a different road because I had to go into Newry. It was around 3 p.m. on a Friday. The route I took had a lot of bends and was very hilly. They weren't major hills, just inclines. But they were big enough that you wouldn't know what was coming from the other side. Even a couple of feet of an incline could mean that you wouldn't see a car coming your way.

I got the phrase in my head again just as I came to the brow of a hill. It was only seconds beforehand. It was a bad piece of road and there was nowhere to go on the sides. I think my guard was down a bit and I was thinking, 'Surely nobody would try to pass on this hill.'

Suddenly a car was coming towards me, on my side of the road. It was overtaking another car which was also coming in the opposite direction to me. The car was going fast. It was one of those situations where you did not have time to react. I had no time to plan or do anything. I didn't even have time to turn the steering-wheel and avoid it.

It all happened so quickly. I saw the driver, like in a flash. He was in his mid-20s to late 20s. I saw his face and for a split second we were eyeball to eyeball. His mouth was open. He looked horrified, shocked and sorry all at the same time. I just had enough time to swear. The only thing that flashed through my mind was, 'Am I going to make it through this?'

Suddenly he was gone. He had grabbed the wheel and he forced his car back in to the left. I don't know how he managed it but we missed each other by inches. It had all happened in a few seconds, just the time it took for me to swear.

He carried on. There was nothing I could have done. It was only because of a reflex action that he had made it. Otherwise we were gone. Had it been a second later we would have smashed into each other. He was so close to the car he was overtaking that he could have hit them as well.

I eventually pulled over, about two minutes later, and I

thought, 'That was it! That was what I was being warned about!' It was that close. It really could have been it. I could have died. I then rang my sister and told her everything – about what I had in my head all day and what had nearly happened.

I think that what took place was confirmation of why the phrase 'Head-on collision!' was coming to me all day. I think that when that car came towards me it crystallised for me, 'This is the moment! This is it!' I really feel I was being forewarned. For me, throughout the early part of that day, the moment was just biding its time.

ANNE, FROM DUBLIN, had a strange preview of her son's battle with cancer. The preview took place in the late 1990s.

My son was aged somewhere between ten and twelve at the time. He was in fine health, like any young boy of his age. He enjoyed playing sports, loved his computer games and was great fun and full of life. He had no worries and was very good at school, where he worked hard and did well. There was no indication of any illness. He only had the minor illnesses that all kids would have, like a bad cold, but that was about it. Life was happy and normal.

One day, during winter, I was on my own at home and was doing a bit of housework. It was around four or five o'clock in the afternoon. I think my son was out with friends and my husband was at work. I recall that it was a Saturday. When I was finished with the housework I went into the living-room, to sit down. I noticed an *Evening Herald* there and I started to read it. I don't know if it was that day's newspaper or whether it was left over from the previous day.

I was flicking through it when I saw a picture of a young boy lying on a sofa. I stopped suddenly. It was a photograph of a boy who was sick. He was lying lengthways along a sofa and he was small enough to be able to fully fit in. I think he was only about seven or eight years old. He didn't look well. His eyes were very tired-looking. Even though it was just a black-and-white photograph, he seemed very pale and ill. He looked worn out.

I then looked at the article and discovered that the boy had died from leukaemia. As I stared at the photo and the article I suddenly said, 'That looks very like my son.' When he was younger he had a habit of lying on a sofa like that. If he was sick he would also snuggle up on the sofa, with a duvet. I got a strong feeling of sadness looking at him.

As I looked at the photograph again, it hit me that it wasn't just a photograph of this other boy – it actually *was* my son! It was almost as if I had flashed forward in time. It was like as if I was looking at a freeze-frame from the future. It wasn't just the picture – it was the feeling I got from it. It was like a realisation or a knowing. From the top of my head down to my toes, I just *knew* it was him.

I looked away and I looked back again and I still knew it. What I felt wasn't logical or anything but it made me very worried and I felt very black. I didn't ask any questions. I didn't say, 'This is ridiculous.' I didn't ask, 'Is my imagination going into overdrive?' I knew it was real and there was no need to question it. I then put the newspaper down and probably even threw it away.

Although I didn't spend the following years worrying about what had happened, it would occasionally cross my mind. I would wonder about it. It wasn't like a cloud over me the whole time, but once a year it would come back to me and I'd think about it. I might be looking at my son and it would return to me. I'd wonder, 'What was that all about?' It was still there. It never left me.

About five, six or seven years later my son was diagnosed with cancer. It came as a total shock, out of the blue. My son was 17 at the time and was a big, strapping lad. He wasn't like the kid in the photograph, who was only around seven or eight. He also got a different type of cancer, not leukaemia. So, in a way, you couldn't entirely match up the photograph with what happened.

Yet there were many parallels. When my son had cancer, he would lie on the sofa. He would have the same kind of feeling about him, of being tired and weary. He also had the look of someone who was fighting a battle that was too big for him and that he wasn't going to win. Sometimes, if I caught him in a certain light or if I looked at him when he wasn't aware I was looking, I could see those things. The feeling from the picture was the same.

In the terror and the shock of absorbing the diagnosis, I didn't immediately match up the photograph with what had happened to my son. But I thought about it shortly afterwards. The picture came into my mind. I said, 'Gosh! I wonder?' It was like a full-screen picture that came flooding back and I thought, 'That's it! That's what I saw!'

My son fought a two-and-a-half-year battle, trying to beat the disease. He didn't win, unfortunately, and he died at the age of 20. Subsequently I wondered, 'Maybe what I felt when I saw the photograph was just the fear every parent has?' When you see a story like that maybe your immediate thought is, 'Oh, my God! Wouldn't it be awful if it happened to my child?' But even when I asked those questions and tried to rationalise it like that, I knew it wasn't true.

I think there was definitely something to what I saw and felt. I don't think it was just a coincidence or an overactive imagination. I certainly think there was a direct connection between the two events. It was also strange that when my son was ill he said, 'I knew I would have to go through something like this.' I said, 'Really?' And he repeated it. But we just left it and I never asked him anymore. I think he felt something too.

I have never experienced anything like it before or since. I also wouldn't be a believer in things like that, in anything supernatural or paranormal. I have never gone to a fortune-teller, nothing like that. I am not gullible. But this was something different, on a completely different level, and it has stayed with me. I still remember seeing the picture, to this day. I can still see myself opening the paper. And I still think about it often, maybe once a month.

I believe that what happened was a premonition. I'm not sure about it being a forewarning, as the word implies that you can do something about it and I never felt I could do that. I hadn't even told anyone because I felt there was no point. But I think I had an image of what lay ahead. I believe I reached into the future for a split second and saw a misty, murky view of the tragedy that was going to happen to my son.

Jonathan, from County Kildare, had a forewarning of a worrying mishap at a funfair. The event happened in January 2009. He was in his late teens at the time.

I had spent about a week around Christmas and New Year persuading one of my close friends to go to the funfair. He absolutely hates amusement rides and roller-coasters and anything like that. He can't stand going on them and never has. He finally agreed to go and so did another friend of mine as well.

The three of us went by train. It was just getting dark as we arrived and the whole place was lit up. People were screaming and shouting on the rides. You could hear the noise coming up the street. The place was packed. We were looking forward to having great fun.

The first thing we saw was this massive roller-coaster that they had outside, with the really big loops. It was the main attraction. I said to my friend, 'Do you want to go on it?' He said, 'No, we'll leave that until the end.' He obviously was scared and didn't want to try it, to begin with. So we went inside, where there were smaller rides, and we went on those first.

About an hour-and-a-half later we came back outside and we said, 'We'll go on the roller-coaster before we leave.' We had been waiting for it and building it up. Although the queue was massive, we lined up anyway. But just when we were getting up to buy the tickets, I got this sinking feeling in my stomach that something was going to happen.

It was a really bad feeling in the pit of my stomach. It wasn't a nervous feeling. I wasn't uptight about going on the roller-coaster because I had been on it a couple of years before that. I wouldn't, anyway, get that sort of sensation before I'd go on a ride. I liked them. What I had was also definitely different from adrenaline.

It was very strange. It was like a sinking feeling telling me, 'Don't go on the ride!' My hands were kind of sweaty. I put it down to being nervous because maybe we had built it up too much. But, underneath, I definitely knew it was something else. I felt something really wrong or bad was going to take place.

I was getting more and more uneasy as we were going up the queue, getting closer to buying the tickets and getting seated on the roller-coaster. I was thinking of my friend as well. I was saying to myself, 'God! Maybe I shouldn't bring him on this ride.' What felt even worse was that I was after convincing him to go on it.

We eventually got to the top of the queue, got the tickets and went on. My friend was saying, 'God! This is going to be really scary!' He was looking forward to it but he was jittery at the same time because he had never been on a big roller-coaster before. I was telling him, 'Oh! It'll be grand. It'll be grand.' But everything seemed to be happening really slowly because I knew that something bad was going to occur.

They put these safety-bars on us and the roller-coaster started going. It went around the first loop and it went around the second loop. It then went to the bottom of it. It was going again for its second journey and I just knew that something awful was coming.

Suddenly there was this big screech and the whole thing came to a halt. It stopped and I was like, 'What's going on?' I could also hear other people, behind us, going, 'God! What's going on? What's going on?'

We were stuck hanging upside down. We were no longer sitting down on the seats. Instead we were pressed against the safety-bars and upended. These metal bars were the only things that kept us from falling. It was uncomfortable. I was thinking, 'Jeez! Are things going to fall out of my pockets?' It was really, really terrifying. It was really cold as well.

One of the things I remember is that I could see all the houses and their back gardens, because we were up so high. I saw swimming-pools in the back gardens. You could see everything that was going on, including all the traffic and the cars. You could hear echoes of all the screams and the laughter from all around the playground.

My friend was in a complete panic. He really started to get scared. He was saying, 'God! Oh, God! Oh, God! Oh, God!' I was trying to calm him down. I was saying to him, 'It's grand. It's probably part of the ride. We'll get off in a few minutes.'

I didn't really believe it myself. I didn't know what was

going to take place. I also had this guilt. I felt, 'If anything happens it will be my fault because it was I who convinced him to go on the roller-coaster.'

We were there for about 15 or 20 minutes. They eventually got it working once again. We came down and when we got off some fellow said, 'Sorry about that, lads. Something just happened there.' He said there was some kind of a technical problem. He didn't explain it too much. And that was it.

We then made the trip home. I was saying, 'Jeez! I got a really bad feeling before I went on that!' My friend said, 'You could have said it! You'd have saved us all the hassle!'

I don't know what it was. It was like something was warning me, 'Don't go on the ride! Don't go on the ride! Don't go on the ride!' It was a bad, bad feeling that something was coming. It could have been my subconscious telling me that something was going to go wrong. My subconscious could have been saying to me, 'Don't get on!' But I really don't know what it was.

You could maybe mistake it for nervousness or adrenaline, especially before going on something like that. But I've had those sorts of sensations before and this was definitely different. It was more of a dark, ominous feeling than nervousness. There is no comparison. This wasn't the same.

It has happened at other times. I would be the sort of person who would get a feeling about something. I would usually get a bad sensation that something is going to occur or that a bad thing is going to happen to somebody. Rarely do I get a good feeling. But this was one of the biggest that I ever experienced. I believe I was definitely forewarned that something was going to take place.

BRENDAN, FROM COUNTY KERRY, sensed that something was wrong with his mother. The year was 1987. He was aged 21.

I was living in Dublin at the time. I was studying there. I woke up one morning, near the end of March, and I had a very vivid sense of my mother. It wasn't that I had been dreaming about her. I just felt that something wasn't right. There was nothing else on my mind when I woke up. I wasn't able to think about anything I had to do on the day. I was just concerned about my mother.

I had no reason to feel this way. I had no idea that anything was amiss. I had no knowledge that my mother was sick or anything. The feeling stayed with me all morning. I even told a fellow-student when I was walking towards the college. I said to him, 'I woke this morning and my mother was very much on my mind. I can't understand it. I can't get her out of my head.'

That evening I got a phone call from home. It was from my sister, who said that my mother wanted to talk to me. I found out then that my mother had just been diagnosed with cervical cancer. My mother said, 'I had a few tests done last week and I have cancer. But there's nothing to be worried about because they have it at the early stages. I'll have to have an operation.' The news I was just getting was suddenly being linked up to the feeling I had that morning.

Up to then there had been no indications that there was anything wrong with my mother. She wasn't looking ill or anything. She just had some problem and went to her GP. She went into hospital very soon after, in the first week of April, and died on 29 April. She died after surgery, having got a massive blood clot. She passed away, aged 47, within a month of her diagnosis.

My aunt – my mother's sister, who lived with us – also had a forewarning of the death. One morning, about three months prior to the diagnosis, my aunt got up and said, 'I had a very funny dream last night. I was sitting by the fire in the sitting-room and my mother and all my brothers and sisters arrived.'

That was my grandmother and my uncles and aunts she was referring to. She named them all. She went through all of them one by one. She said, 'What were they coming for?' She couldn't understand what the dream was about and why they were all coming into the house. That dream happened around January.

My aunt was at home, four months later, on the day that my mother died. She was sitting by the fire. Suddenly, after the news emerged that my mother had passed away, all of these people started to come in. They started arriving and gathering at the house. There was her mother and her brothers and sisters – that's my grandmother and uncles and aunts. 'That's my dream! They are here!' my aunt said. She had seen them all coming.

I feel, looking back, that maybe there is some sort of spiritual connection where you are forewarned or prepared in some way. We know so little about our minds and how they work. The mind can contain memories for 40 or 100 years so maybe it can also reach out into the future or reach other people and ascertain what's happening with them. I just don't know. But what happened has always stayed with me. It's comforting in some ways too.

ANNA, WHO NOW LIVES IN COUNTY MEATH, had two premonitions back in the early 1990s. Her home, at the time, was on the border between County Dublin and County Kildare.

Twenty-one years ago, in summertime, I was travelling home

in my car. It was late, around midnight. I was driving on my own. I was coming up the brow of a hill within 150 yards of my home. It was very familiar territory to me. Although I was well back from the brow of the hill, I knew I was going to hit something. I just *knew* it. I was certain. I felt terror and fear. It was absolutely horrible.

I looked everywhere but I couldn't see anything I was going to hit. There was nothing on the road yet I felt terrified inside. I couldn't understand where this came from. The feeling was so strong that I pulled over to the side of the road and stopped the car. I felt so bad that I actually stopped on an empty road.

I eventually drove off and went home. It only took me seconds because I was that close. When I drove in I could see a light on in a window. My daughter was there and I thought I'd go up and tell her what happened. So I went up and said it to her. She talked to me and calmed me down. I was still terribly upset.

I eventually got over it and went to bed. I forgot about it and that was the end of that. The next evening, however, I was coming home from work. This was around teatime, about six o'clock. At exactly the same spot there was a slight blockage of traffic. Cars had slowed down because there was a crash at the brow of the hill. The driver of a car, who I discovered later was about 30 years old, was covered with a jacket – someone had put it over him – and he was dead in his car.

It seems that the driver had been overtaking another car as he travelled up to the brow of the hill. He obviously didn't see a lorry which was coming from the opposite direction. It wasn't a full head-on. The lorry had done its best to avoid him. It had gone up a bank, into a garden hedge. The car, when I saw it, was beyond the lorry. It was still on the road, badly damaged on the driver's side and he was dead.

The driver obviously took a risk that didn't work out. He must have known he was going to hit the lorry, just as I knew I was going to hit something. It shook me up. I came home again, just as I did the night before, and this time I said to my daughter, 'There's a man dead just down the road.' I would probably have never said anything about it if I hadn't told her the night before.

Afterwards I really puzzled about what had happened and about our understanding of time. Somehow, 18 hours before the accident, I had felt that man's fear. I had picked it up. He had absolutely nothing to do with me. He was single, somebody's son, and he came from elsewhere. Yet I felt his fear. I have no doubt about that. I am convinced that's what I felt, that absolute all-consuming terror. That's my conviction.

The second event happened about a year later. I was up in Donegal, taking a break at the end of the summer. The children had gone back to school and I was taking a week off. I was on my own, in a cottage. I woke up, one night, at about half-two in the morning. I thought I heard something.

I was filled with apprehension, thinking that there was somebody downstairs. I was terrified because I thought I was in danger. It took me about 15 minutes to realise that I wasn't in danger, that there was nobody downstairs and that I was alone.

I was still terrified but I knew it wasn't me who was in danger, it was somebody else. I just knew. I felt I knew who it was. I thought he was in some sort of physical danger. Even though it was now half-two or a quarter-to-three in the morning, I went downstairs. I walked down the metal spiral staircase to get to the phone. There were no mobile phones at that time. So I went to the landline and I rang the person in question.

He answered the phone and I told him, 'Be careful! I think

there's something terribly wrong! I think something is going to happen!' He just said, 'Thanks.' That was about all. There was no conversation of any length. I then went back to bed. The next evening I rang him again. The first thing he said to me was, 'How did you know?' I said, 'I don't know. I just woke up thinking that something was going to happen.'

It then transpired that he had very big trouble at work that day. It wasn't physical danger and there was no physical attack, but it was a very big work issue that he had known was coming but it hadn't happened yet. He knew it was coming and it did happen. It happened in the morning, not long after I had phoned him.

He couldn't understand how I knew. He couldn't explain how I was ringing up and saying, 'Be careful! I think there's something terribly wrong!' I also can't explain it. I never knew of this issue he had at work before. I had no inkling of it. I don't know what happened or how I felt he was in danger. It's just that I know I was frightened for him.

I am aware, looking back, that both events were odd. They were strange and they have stayed with me. It's not that I think about them much. But when people are relating stories of their own, I might tell them of the man who died in the crash. I tell it more in the context of how little we know about time.

What is time? How did I take up his fear? How did I do so even before he had experienced it himself? The fear was horrendous. I have never been frightened like that about any situation ever since. Even now, when I talk about it, I feel bad inside. I don't think I have ever experienced such terror in real life and I hope I never go through anything like it again.

TOM, FROM COUNTY CORK, developed a feeling that his daughter had become pregnant against all the odds.

We thought my daughter had leukaemia, and she had to go into hospital. Specialists examined her and carried out tests. They found out that her problem wasn't leukaemia at all but that the platelets in her blood were dropping very low. She was fine but, now and again, she had to get her platelets looked after. Above all, however, the specialists came to the conclusion that, because of the root cause of the problem, she would never have children.

She came home from hospital and I was a bit upset. She was the youngest and a bit special. Her local doctor asked her, 'Do you want to have counselling?' Her attitude was, 'Look! If this is God's will, that's it, there's nothing I can do about it.'

A few years passed by and my daughter had entered a relationship. She was living with her partner. One night I was supposed to go to meet her for tea. I had a bad day at work. I said to my wife, 'I can't meet her. I'm too tired. Tell her I'll meet up on Saturday.' However, on my way home from work, the strangest thing happened to me. As I was coming into our local village, my niece – my brother's daughter – was walking up the street with her baby.

I rolled the window down and gave her a wave. She waved back and said, 'Hello!' But as she waved back I suddenly found that I wasn't looking at my niece but at my own young daughter. 'That's the strangest thing!' I said. I had never seen a resemblance between them, yet it was just like my own daughter looking back at me.

It was almost like you would see on the television when someone is going into a dream sequence. They use a sort of ripple effect to show what's happening. It was almost like that. The feeling was most strange. I felt it was very weird. I wondered was I tired. Nothing beyond that registered with me at that stage.

I drove home and sat down. I was on my own, lying on the couch and having a bit of a sleep. At around eight o'clock the phone rang. I jumped up and immediately knew, 'That's my daughter and she's going to tell me she is pregnant!' I just *knew* it. Bang! I had it straight away.

I went to the phone and my daughter said, 'Where are you?' I said, 'Did you get my message?' She said, 'I have a bit of news for you.' I said to her, 'I know, and I already love your child!' My granddaughter is now aged nine.

I think she thought that I would be upset with her being pregnant because she was in a live-in relationship but wasn't married. But that wasn't so at all. I was delighted. I was thrilled. And I had actually known. The very moment the phone rang, everything had clicked into place.

Since then my little granddaughter has asked me where she comes from. I have a story I tell her about how I was bold when I was a little boy and how I then got a wish for being good. It's a big story that I tell her. So I took her out and showed her the night sky. I showed her the middle star in Orion. I told her, 'I was once given that star to wish on and I wished on that star and I was given you.'

I have also told her that she is a real Celtic princess. There was a downside to that. She was in school, some years ago, and the teacher was giving out to her for some reason. She put her hand up and said, 'Excuse me, Miss! You're not to give out to me! Do you know that I was got by a wish on a star and I'm a real Celtic princess?' She's my pride and joy. And, although she was totally unexpected, she has a brother now.

I have also had premonitions about my contacting other people or other people contacting me. My uncle, for example, lives on the Aran Islands. I often wake up in the morning and say, 'I must phone him today.' Almost every time that happens, he then phones me that night. I end up saying, 'You were on my mind today and I was thinking about phoning you.' Sometimes I say to him, 'I wish you had been my father because we are so alike.'

I'm the same with my sister. We are very close. I often come home and phone her and she would say to me, 'I was just going to phone you. You were on my mind all day.' It's amazing. I'd sometimes meet someone after thinking about them. I'd walk around the corner and there they are. I can never really explain that at all.

I also have a brother and sister who are twins. Both live and work in England, one in London, the other in York. The male twin could ring up his twin sister and say, 'Listen! You'd want to cheer yourself up today, because whatever is going on in your head is getting me down.'

It's the same with her. If anything is going on with her twin brother she seems to know it. They are unbelievable. They can sense what's going on with each other. It's the most amazing thing.

I wonder, in those cases, if it is that family members have so much in common. There's a connection there. I think that might be the same in most families. There's a link, an understanding. We are the sum total of our parents and we are part of each other. That connection is always there.

But the story regarding my daughter is different. I have a great belief, in that case, in the 'Divine'. I'm a Roman Catholic by birth and I hope I'm a good Christian. I'm not a Bible-pusher but I honestly believe that there is a 'Divine' and part of it is in us. At times it opens and we can see. At those times we use our 'Divine intellect'. I really believe that.

I remember, one time, talking to a guy about painting. I said, 'I can sometimes be painting and I don't realise it's me.'

He said, 'That happens to me too.' He then went on to say, 'Something in our head opens up like a door and the energy flows both ways when you are on a roll.' I believe, in other words, that there's something greater than us all. I'm sure of that.

Mark, from County Westmeath, has had forewarnings of many future events.

The first one I had, in the presence of somebody else, took place in the early 2000s. I was driving from the Midlands to Ballinasloe, just to visit somebody. My sister was in the car with me, in the passenger seat. I was passing a garage and there was a big sign blocking an exit.

I suddenly saw a car coming out from the garage really, really fast. Whoever was driving it was going too quick and they didn't look to see if anyone was coming. Trying not to hit it, I jammed on the brakes and I didn't hit the car. I nearly did but I had braked on time. I then drove on.

Ten seconds later my sister started crying. I asked her, 'What's wrong?' She said that ten seconds earlier she saw me driving down the road. It was a perfectly-clear road, with no one coming out, nothing wrong. She saw me jam on the brakes, for no reason, in the middle of the road. As the car came to a stop, I put it back in first gear and drove nice and slow. Then, all of a sudden, this car flew out from the side of the road. But that was about ten seconds or so later.

What had happened was that I had seen the car before it ever tried to come out on the road. I saw it ten seconds earlier, before the whole thing happened. I didn't even realise this. It was only after she said it to me that I realised what had gone on.

I know, if I had kept driving, I would have crashed into the car at an awful pace. The driver never looked my way at all and no doubt we would have had a collision and someone would have died. Then I told my sister. I said, 'I have these things all the time.' She was the first person I told.

Around three or four weeks after the car scenario, I was going to see my brother. My sister had told him what had happened. He said, 'OK! Let's see if this really works!' He got a pack of 52 cards. He spread them out on the floor and said, 'Let's find the four of diamonds.'

He asked me to point at the wrong ones first and to take them away. I took away 51 cards and the one I left behind was the four of diamonds. I was doing this just to entertain him but, to be honest, it frightened the hell out of me and I haven't done it since.

When I was a child I assumed this sort of thing happened to everybody. The first time it happened was when I was two-and-a-half. I was in my own home and my grandfather was visiting. I bit him on the lip and it was bleeding, yet nobody gave out to me for it. I was in the sitting-room when this happened. But when I walked out to the kitchen I realised that it hadn't happened at all.

What had occurred was that I had seen it in my head and I recognised that nobody had given out to me. I didn't know what was going on but as a kid I couldn't believe that I got away with it. So I said, 'I'll go back in and bite his lip now.'

I went back in and bit him on the lip, to see would somebody say anything to me. It started bleeding in the exact same way. And nothing was said, nobody gave out to me. That's the first memory I have of it happening. It has stuck with me to this day.

Throughout my life, since then, it has happened all the time. Only a few weeks ago I was meeting two friends in a pub, to watch a Premier League football match. It was on a Sunday and I was running slightly late. When I came into the bar I saw my friend telling our other friend that the score was one-nil and the team had scored in the first minute. But when I sat down and looked up, the score was nil-all.

I said, 'What the hell is going on here? The score is one-nil!' I went to the toilet straight away and when I came back our other mate was only in the process of sitting down and my friend was telling him that a goal had just been scored, in the first minute, and it was one-nil!

I can think of other examples. I work in quality control with a company. My job is to make sure that everything runs smoothly and everything that goes out is perfect. If there is a problem, one of the operators will alert me about what is happening and we will fix it. About 20 per cent of the time I'm down in the area before the problem even happens.

I am sometimes just taking a walk around the floor, to see what is going on. I stop somewhere and something goes wrong. I might even have the relevant paperwork with me. There's a running gag that I'm a jinx and something happens while I'm there. But it's the other way around. I'm just ready for something but I don't realise it.

I can think of another example similar to that. If I close the door of my car it locks, so I could lock my keys inside. I obviously try not to do that. But, occasionally, I have got into my car, driven off a bit but then come back to the house and gone to the press and got the spare key to my car.

I then put the spare key in my back pocket and get back in my car and head off again to wherever I was going. Three hours later I come out and realise I have left my keys in the car. I start panicking but I then put my hand in my back pocket and find the spare key. That has happened more than once.

I can sometimes be in company and it happens too. I can be sitting in a room where people are talking. It could be family and they are talking away when I call in on a Sunday. I know what's going to happen in the conversation and who is going to say what, word for word. Someone might come in and say something that I didn't expect. But, generally, I can see where the conversation is going.

Occasionally it results in me being a bit short with people, especially when I know exactly what they are going to say. Even when they cannot explain it, I know what they are thinking. I feel they have already told me what they are saying.

Also on the family front, I was recently at a funeral. On the way home I said to my sister, 'Our uncle will be dead very soon!' He was a big, strong man but I just knew. He was telling a joke and everyone was laughing but I looked into his eyes. I thought, 'Oh, no!' I got a pain in my stomach for the pain I knew that his family would feel when he died. He died a few weeks afterwards.

There is another common example which happens a lot. It's a Friday evening and I decide to go for a drink with some friends. I would be at the bar, ordering drinks. I would see a guy sitting at the bar. I would think, 'Oh, no! This guy is in trouble!' I would never have seen him before in my life. At the end of the night, when I would get a taxi home, he would be lying down on the ground in trouble.

If I walk past somebody that I have never seen before in my life, nine times out of ten I can tell if they are sad or happy. I don't want to know that and I'm not trying. I don't even know them but I just know what's going on. Even at work if I see someone walking by or moving I can tell what's wrong. Nine times out of ten what I think is wrong is wrong. And it's not just that I *think* something is wrong – I *know* what it is that is wrong.

There have been loads of times when things like that have happened. If I walk into a shop I might see someone in front of me. I don't see their aura or anything like that. But I can tell if they are sad or nervous. If I see two of my friends and one has cheated on the other one, I just seem to know. I know, by looking at them, that something is wrong and I will know what it is. I just *know*.

The only people who I have told about this are my sister and brother and one friend. But I think everybody in my family knows. Whenever they talk about horse-racing they say things like, 'Get Mark in here.' But it doesn't work that way. It isn't like that.

I don't 'do' this. I don't sit down and think. It just comes into my head and that's it. It has never helped me anytime I wanted it to help me. I know if I went into Paddy Power's to lay a bet it wouldn't work for me at all.

When it happens to me it is absolutely random. If I am walking down the street it's not that I say, 'Let me think what is going on with the person in front of me.' I don't care about the people but I know straight away. Sometimes it's just a feeling. It doesn't worry me but I feel it gives me an advantage at times.

I think everybody has the potential to see what I see. There are just so many things going on – you are going to work, you are busy, you are watching television, and nobody listens to anything at all. If you sat down for five minutes, and collected yourself, I think anyone would be able to do it.

If you just gave yourself time to think and listen to what your inner-self or subconscious is saying, nine times out of ten it would tell you what you would need to know. I think I am better than some people at this but not nearly as good as others. Yet I definitely think everybody can do it, it's just that they don't try.

DENISE, FROM COUNTY KERRY, recalls what happened at the exact time her grandfather died. The sad event took place in the mid-1990s, when she was aged 11.

My granddad came to visit and spent the weekend at our house. He was my mother's father and I was very fond of him. He was a very nice man. We usually visited him but on this occasion he came to us. His wife was in hospital at the time. It was the only occasion I ever remember him staying over in our house. I think he came on a Saturday evening and he stayed in my sister's bedroom. There was no sign that he was sick or unwell.

I had school on the Monday morning. I was in primary school. Our school was very small, with only about 100 pupils in all and about 12 in my class. I used to sit at the top of the classroom, right in front of the teacher's desk. I think we might have been having Irish class and waiting for the break at 11 o'clock. I was looking forward to break-time. I mustn't have been paying attention to what was going on.

A thought suddenly came into my head. I wondered, 'What would happen if my granddad died in my sister's bedroom? Wouldn't that be awful?' It was a very vivid thought. It was strange because, being so young, I wouldn't have been thinking about death. It knocked me sideways. It wasn't a normal thing to come into my head.

I thought, 'That's a silly thing to be thinking of. Where did that come from?' It wasn't nice to be thinking about it. I didn't know where it originated and I hated it. It was scary. But somehow, at that moment, I was worried that my granddad would die in our house and that frightened me.

We had our break and went back to class as usual. After lunchtime our local priest came into the classroom and started chatting to my teacher at the top of the room. I presumed that he was dealing with either confirmation or communion or something like that. I later found out that he was talking about my granddad, although nothing was said to me at the time.

I didn't find out what had happened to my granddad until around the time that class ended at 3 o'clock. My dad came to collect me. It was very strange that he was outside waiting for me. I normally used to walk home from school or get a lift home with somebody. But, on that day, he was there and he told me that my granddad had died that morning.

I remember my dad put his arms around me as he told me. I think I said, 'What? When did it happen?' At that moment I remember linking the thought that I had earlier with my granddad's death. But I didn't say anything to my dad. I said it instead to my mum around the time of the funeral. She was intrigued by what I told her. She asked me, 'What do you mean?' I explained to her exactly what had happened and what I had thought about.

I eventually found out what time my granddad had died. He had died just before 11 o'clock. It was the exact same time that I was thinking about him and wondering what would happen if he passed away. I think he died suddenly from a problem with his heart. It hadn't happened in the bedroom. It had happened instead in the kitchen. But he had died and his death took place at the same time as I was thinking about him.

It seems that my granddad had come to the kitchen to have his breakfast. My mum was cooking it. My little brother was there also. My mum was saying, 'It's a lovely day' or something like that. Her back was turned to him. When she looked over he was sitting in the chair but his head was slumped. The doctor came and he was immediately pronounced dead.

I had some dreams, later on, of my granddad. In one of

them I was standing in the kitchen and looking down the hallway towards my bedroom, which I could see from the kitchen. My granddad was sitting on the bed and was beckoning me with his finger. That kind of scared me. I had another where someone was at the window and wanted to be let in. I was nervous about that too. Those dreams came to me for a while afterwards, over the space of a few months. And then they stopped.

What happened on the day my granddad died was strange. Nobody, at the time, was talking about him being ill. I also didn't think about things like that back then. But maybe it happened to me because I was young. You always hear that children are more open to things like this. And even though what occurred wasn't good, it was nice to know that I was thinking about him when he was dying.

What took place comes back to me often enough. I like to think that it was my granddad's way of saying goodbye. I think he wanted somebody to remember him so he came to me. Maybe he was scared and wanted to be with someone. Perhaps he was sending a message to me. Whatever it was, it was a real feeling. I can still recall it clearly and I can still see myself sitting in the class. The memory of what happened has never left me and probably never will.

JAMES, FROM NORTHERN IRELAND, has an extraordinary ability to foresee the future.

One thing that stands out in my mind happened when I was working on the grass verge of a major motorway. We were landscaping. There were 12 of us on the side of the road. The boss was in the depot, about three miles away. I got a premonition that he was coming down the road to check on us. I turned to the guy beside me and I said, 'The boss is on the way down. I know he's coming.' He shouted to the lads. The next minute the jeep came around the bend.

The guys later said, 'You must have known that he was coming.' I said, 'I got an inkling that he was on his way.' It's weird how it happens. It just pops into your head. It's a strong and warm feeling. I could actually see the boss physically getting into the jeep. I could feel his movements almost to the second. It's both a sense and a vision. It's both of them together to the extent that you can almost feel emotional about it.

The lads couldn't believe it. They asked me, 'How did you do that?' I said, 'I don't know how I do it. I just do it and that's it.' They said, 'That was only a stroke of luck. Do it again another time.' Hours later, that same day, I said, 'He's coming again.' They said, 'Oh, right! You're winding us up.' He came around the corner again. That was an example of where I was having fun with it.

On a different occasion I was about to go to Belfast with a friend. It was early in the morning. Before I left the house I stopped and said, 'We're going to have to delay a while.' My friend asked, 'Why?' I said, 'Because something is going to happen. I don't know what it is but I fear for my life. Let's hang around the house for a while and then we'll go.' He said, 'OK! Let's have a quick cup of tea.' That's what we did and five or six minutes later we got in the car and left.

After driving for about three or four miles, we approached a T-junction. A van suddenly came from another road onto our road, right in front of us. I slammed my foot on the brakes. I did it so hard that I actually damaged the disc in the front wheel.

My friend looked at me and I looked at him. I said, 'That's why we paused back at the house. Otherwise he would have been stuck into the side of us.' I found out later that the van had been coming towards the T-junction and the driver had seen us coming but he couldn't stop. It was like his brakes didn't function temporarily.

I can think of another one that happened in the car. I was approaching a particular bend and I slowed the car down almost to a stop. I said to my wife, 'There's a crash around the corner.' She said, 'How do you know?' I said, 'You'll see in a second.' We came around the corner and there was a car on its roof. No one was killed or anything. But I had seen the accident ahead.

A similar thing happened when my wife and I were in a nearby town to do a bit of shopping. A friend of my wife's had supposedly gone to England. Yet I turned to my wife in the car park and said, 'Your friend is here.' I said, 'She's going to be pulling in right beside us, any second now, in her car.'

My wife said, 'That's going to be hard because she's over in England.' My feeling was getting stronger and stronger and I said, 'No, she's going to pull in any second now.' The next minute, exactly as I predicted, her friend's car pulled in and she was in it with her kids. She had cancelled her trip to England.

Another time my sister had come on a visit from where she lives up to Northern Ireland. She stayed the night. The next morning, as she was getting in the car, all I could see was water. Just for a split second I could see water and a leak. It hit me straight over the head. I went up to her and said, 'When you get home, call a plumber.' She said, 'Why is that?' I said, 'You have a leak at home but it's not that bad, everything is going to be OK.' She started laughing.

Later on that day the phone jingled. It was my sister. 'No way!' she said. 'I can't believe that you could have known that!' I said, 'Known what?' She said, 'The pipe at the back of the washing-machine is after coming away and the floor is soaked.' She knew what I could do. She asked me, 'What did you see or feel?' I told her, 'Just as you were about to go, my mind focused on your house and I could see water about an inch deep.'

The things that happen are mostly bad. Sometimes it can be a case of the hair standing up on the back of my neck. I have, for example, often brushed off a person and got flashes or visions of their lives. I get a rush for just a couple of seconds. I might know they are going to die a painful death. That could happen when I am walking up the road and someone is beside me. It could happen at mass or walking down the street in town. That can be very scary.

Sometimes the things that happen occur within minutes, sometimes in hours, sometimes it takes a year. Sometimes they can be useful, especially from the point of view of my self-preservation. There are numerous instances where I have decided to do something, or not to do something, to change the future. In that sense it has protected me. It's like some sort of built-in mechanism which can help me. It has worked perfectly, so far.

I am very careful who I talk to about it. People might go, 'That's weird!' But I have told some people, including my mother. I told her, 'I can sometimes see things before they happen.' She used to have this ability too, although maybe not as strong. She said, 'Tell nobody. Keep it to yourself or they may not understand.'

I have occasionally found that what she said is right, that people think you are strange and steer clear. So, mostly, I just keep it to myself. But I definitely can foretell the future and can sense it and see it as well. I know there's something there and there's something to it, without a shadow of a doubt. And I definitely believe that people do have an extra sense.

JOHN, FROM COUNTY CARLOW, felt an urge to pray for a woman at exactly the time she died.

I had a very good friend of mine who lived just beside us and was a great friend of the family's. She was a great old neighbour and a lovely woman. She was very straight and very down-to-earth, very honest. A few years ago she was in hospital, suffering from old age. She was in her 80s and had been sick for a while. I knew she was deteriorating and nobody expected her to pull through.

I was up in the garden, one afternoon during the summer, doing a bit of digging. I remember it was a beautiful, fine summer's day. I was sowing potatoes or something like that, in great form. I was busy doing it when I just started thinking of the woman. She came into my mind.

It was around half-two at the time. I said to myself, 'I'll take time out at three o'clock and I'll say a prayer for her. I'll finish up before that and leave the tools back up in the shed and say the prayer for her there.'

I don't know why I chose three o'clock. I just picked it and said it to myself. So, just coming up to three o'clock, I went up to the shed and sat down. I blessed myself and said a Hail Mary and an Our Father and finished with the end prayer of the Rosary. I know I said the prayers at three o'clock.

I was coming out of the shed when my wife emerged from the back door of the house and called me. The house is about 30 or 40 yards away. She said she had just got a phone call telling her that the woman was after passing away. She was just after dying. At the time my wife told me, it was shortly after three o'clock.

I later asked the woman's family what time she had passed away and one of the members of the family told me that it was three o'clock exactly. The person I spoke to was sure of the time. Apparently, at the end, she had died of old age. Her heart had just given up.

I was shocked, in a way, and I found it strange but not that strange. I asked myself was it coincidence? Or what was it? I believe there was some connection there. I know she was sick but I wasn't to know that she would die at three o'clock on the day that I prayed for her. I believe I had some feeling that something was happening, that I was tuned in. There was a feeling of warmth there.

I am happy about what happened in the sense that I said the prayer as she was dying. It makes me feel good that I was thinking of her and she was thinking of me at exactly that time. It's amazing, though, how these things happen. As it says in the Bible, we're only allowed to know so much.

KATE, FROM COUNTY ANTRIM, has had a number of textbook premonitions at various times in her life.

The one that stands out most in my life happened when I was 17, over three decades ago. My uncle had been unwell with psychological problems, which he had for a very long time. Otherwise he was physically well. I always kept in touch with him and he had occasionally come to stay with us for the weekend. We had gone to visit him too.

Suddenly, out of nowhere, I had this 'dread'. It was a sensation of fear and anxiety. I would go to bed at night wondering what it meant. I would be unable to sleep. I couldn't quite put my finger on what was causing it. I just knew that something was going to happen. It was a horrible sensation and was pretty much there all the time over a few months. It followed me around everywhere.

One Saturday evening two policemen arrived at the door of our house. This wasn't a normal thing to happen. I immediately knew, 'That's it! This is what I have been worrying about, what I have been dreading!' Even though they didn't at first say that my uncle was dead, I knew that's what had happened. I was instantly aware that he had died. I knew that's what I had been expecting, although I couldn't have known it was going to happen.

Everything suddenly fell into place and the feeling of dread left me. Although I still had the grief you would have after being bereaved, I didn't have the fearful sensation anymore. It was suddenly hit in the head. It was a complete relief. But I couldn't have known that my uncle was going to die. If I had known at the time that this dread was about someone's death, my uncle would never have come within my radar. I would have probably thought it was about my parents.

Nine years later I experienced the exact same sensations – the dread, the anxiety and the worrying that something bad was going to happen. It wasn't a sense of depression – I never had that. It was an intense, ominous fear of what was coming. This time it was even worse because I had experienced it before. Everything was heightened because I felt that something was going to occur. I knew it wasn't going to be very pleasant. The only thing I didn't know about was the how, when or where.

I was in my mid-20s, at that stage, and was living away from home. I had come home one weekend and was in bed. I woke on the Saturday morning to the sound of my mum calling my name and I knew straight away that there was trouble. I instantly recognised that this was what the anxiety had been about. I sprang from my bed. She had collapsed in the bathroom and had a brain haemorrhage. She died the next day.

I just knew from the minute I woke up and heard her voice calling me that, 'This is what I have been waiting for! This is what I feared!' That was my first really bad experience of bereavement and the grief that's involved. Yet the sense of dread instantly disappeared. Once again the fear was gone. There was that sense of release. It was as if the last piece of the jigsaw was put into place.

It happened a third time, when I was in my 40s. This time it concerned my dad. It was the very same thing again, that ominous feeling of dread. Shortly afterwards my dad was diagnosed with stomach cancer. I had the feeling in the lead up to the diagnosis. I had sensed something was coming. He died a few months later.

What happened with my dad didn't cause me as much anxiety. I possibly had a better idea of who it was about, maybe because my dad was old, in his early 80s. I probably associated how I was feeling with him, although he was in good health leading up to the diagnosis and I couldn't have known what was coming.

I wonder sometimes if the whole thing started when I was much younger. Just before I was eight years of age my granny died. We had been very close. I remember not being able to sleep, night after night after night. I had this same fear. I was having a terrible time, watching the hands of the clock going around and around all night and not sleeping.

I was worrying about I don't know what. I remember getting out of my bed and standing beside my parents' bed so that I could have some contact with them. I was that frightened. What I felt was similar to the dread I felt later in my life. But I can't place whether I felt that way before or after my granny passed away.

I'd love to be able to know at what stage I felt that way – before or after she died – but no one is alive now to tell me. I know that if the fear happened beforehand, I would be concerned about it. I would be frightened. If it happened after she died it would be a natural thing to occur.

This feeling of dread – that something is definitely going to take place – never happened at other times in my life. I've never had it since. That time with my dad was the last occasion. I also haven't spoken about it with many people, although I did tell my husband and he was very understanding. He didn't think it was weird or anything.

I don't know what the experiences are. Do we have some sort of 'sixth sense'? Do we have feelings about what's ahead? Do we have foresight? I just don't know. But they are obviously forewarnings of some kind. They tell us that something is going to befall us, involving somebody close. That something then happens.

The brain is obviously a fantastic piece of machinery. Sometimes, out of the blue, it does strange things. Images occasionally come into my head about things way in the past that have no bearing on anything. Then there are those feelings of the future, which I'm glad are gone. I would be very frightened and concerned if I felt them again. I'd certainly see them as a warning that something bad was going to happen and that wouldn't be good.

BRÍD, FROM COUNTY CLARE, has had premonitions since her late teens. She describes a selection of them, both good and bad.

One of the premonitions I had involved a car crash. My daughter, who was in her teens, was playing a match and I drove her to it. It was on a Saturday and we were travelling along the road, on our way home. We suddenly passed a house. There was another house further up. A guy came out from one house in a car and he pulled into the other house. He was a young lad, obviously driving his first car.

I said to my daughter, 'If you ever want to imagine Daddy when he was 18 or 19, that's what he would have been like.'

It was like someone would be after they bought a first car. They'd be going from this friend's house to that friend's house. I said, 'That's exactly what Daddy would have been doing.' We were laughing about it.

I suddenly thought, 'Oh, my God! I hope they will be careful tonight!' I don't know why it came into my head. Then the thought was gone, just as quickly. I drove on and soon arrived at the main road. I turned right. Had I turned left I would have come to the scene of a very bad accident that happened a long time ago. A car had gone on fire and the driver died.

Just as I turned right that old accident came back into my head. It had been dormant in my head for years. I was suddenly convinced there was going to be another accident. It was like as if a dark cloud had descended on the place. I had this awful feeling of doom and gloom. The feeling was really terrible. It was a quivery feeling and not very nice. It was like as if I was not in this world.

I said to my daughter, 'I hope there won't be an accident tonight!' I kept going, although I wanted to stop. I came to a shop and said to my daughter, 'Let's go in here and get an ice-cream.' She just looked at me because she knew I never liked ice-cream. I said, 'We'll get one for the youngest fellow too.' So we stopped and the feeling evaporated.

I went to mass the next morning. It was a Sunday in mid-summer. We went to 12 o'clock mass, which was unusual for us. The priest came out onto the altar. The first thing he said was, 'Last night I was called urgently to the hospital. Three young fellows were in a car crash and died.' He went on to say how he had to tell the parents and how they had to be wakened at three o'clock or four o'clock in the morning to be told. I thought, 'Oh, my God!'

I wondered where the crash had happened. As I came out

of the church I heard a person say where it had occurred. It turned out that the three lads had been driving on the same road I had been on and had been killed close to the spot where I had sensed that something would happen. It was very near the place where I had come out onto the main road, just a couple of minutes away. I nearly got sick.

I have had many other premonitions over the years. I remember, for example, being at home one Friday afternoon. It was before the recycling rubbish started to be collected. Instead there was a place where you could drop the stuff off. I thought, 'I'll get rid of all the recycling stuff before the weekend. I'll take it up to the place and then collect the lads from school.'

As I was going outside with the bags I thought, 'I don't think I'll do that. I'll wait until tomorrow morning.' So I went back in and brought the bags with me. It was like something sent me back with the bags. Then I thought, 'No, we're going somewhere in the morning and I don't want to be delayed. I'll do it now.' So off I went again and took the bags.

After I had delivered them I was heading back out onto the main road. As I was about to go around a corner didn't this huge juggernaut come around it from the other direction. The driver cut the bend. His lorry came right in on top of me. I said, 'Oh, my God!' I thought, 'This is it!' I kind of went into shock. I stopped the car and got out. I said, 'Thank God, I'm alive!'

The juggernaut had totally destroyed the mudguard of my car and the wheel at the front. The bodywork was gone in places. I told the driver he had given me an awful fright but he said, 'I didn't even see you.' I immediately knew that the feeling I had earlier was a warning that something was about to happen. Unfortunately I ignored it and I shouldn't have. It was definitely telling me not to go.

The premonitions can sometimes be good. I have a friend and I met her one day. She said to me, 'I've got something to say to you.' I said, 'OK!' She said, 'I got a call from my brother and he is going on a cruise with his wife.' They were getting a flight from Dublin and then joining up with the cruise. She hadn't been getting on with her brother for a while. She felt something was going to go badly wrong.

As she was speaking I was looking at her. I was away in a sort of trance. The feeling suddenly struck me that everything was going to be alright. It was like a vibe that everything was going to be perfect. I was certain that there was not going to be a plane crash. I was sure everything was going to be good between them again. As it turned out the cruise was grand, everything was absolutely fine, and since then they have re-established contact. It's only a small thing but everything worked out.

Another small one happened regarding hens that we have, which my husband is very attached to. My husband had gone out in the car and I was looking out the window. I saw the hens walking about. I suddenly thought, 'Something is going to happen to them!' I rang my husband and said, 'Hurry back and get those hens into their house.'

When he came back he found that one of the hens was missing. He and my son were broken-hearted. So was I. That night, however, I knew it was all going to be fine. I just *knew* it. I jumped up in the bed and I said to my husband, 'Don't worry. The hen will be back tomorrow. It will be there in the morning.' It was like I had a feeling of elation.

I wasn't just consoling him. It was a feeling I got. With all the trees and wildlife surrounding us, he said there wasn't a hope the hen was going to survive. He thought I was just consoling him and he was saying that the hen wouldn't be back.

I'm a very early riser and the moment I opened the door the next morning the hen ran out of the bushes. I was so delighted I ran back into the house and showed them the hen. I know it's a small story but I *knew* the hen would be fine.

I suppose that I could describe what I get as 'feelings'. Sometimes I get a feeling of elation. It's like something comes up from your feet. It's like a wave coming up through your body. You are calm, at peace and it's a happy feeling. But that's when what happens is going to be good. It's all the happier if it concerns someone else and that you are helping someone.

When it's a bad feeling it can be awful. It's not very nice. It really is doom and gloom. It's a feeling that all is not right and that you are in a very wrong, dark place. When it happens, if I am talking to someone, I wouldn't know what they are saying. I wouldn't hear them. I'd be away in another world. If I got the feeling in the car, and the radio was on, I wouldn't hear the song. I'd only hear what's going on in my head.

I don't know what they are and I have often wondered, 'Are they a bad thing or a good thing?' They frighten me at times. Sometimes I just want to cry. But I don't get them as much as I used to. And I think they are all warnings. They are feelings that something is going to happen. The only good thing is that when the feeling happens it leaves as quickly as it comes. It's gone like a shot.

Tommy, from County Wexford, has had experiences involving his young daughter and some former school friends.

The first story dates back to the late 1960s. My wife and I were between houses at the time. We had sold our old house and bought another house but there was a mix-up in the timing. My wife decided to bring our two children over to

England, to visit her sister. I had to stay in Ireland because I had to work. I went back to stay with my parents. My wife went to England for a fortnight but the visit lasted for two months until we could sort things out.

One Monday night, during this time, I was playing cards with my mother and some visitors. There were four of us sitting around a small table in the kitchen. Suddenly, at about a quarter-to-nine, I thought I heard my daughter give a little cry. She was about four years old at the time. The whimper seemed to be coming from upstairs. But my daughter was in England. I put it down to my subconscious mind missing my family.

Twice more, in the next 30 or 40 minutes, the same thing happened again. I heard the same little whimper or cry. It sounded like a child crying upstairs. It was almost like a child was whimpering when turning over in the bed or something like that. I again said to myself that it must have been my subconscious missing my family. No one else heard anything.

Then, at approximately quarter-to-ten, I heard my daughter's voice so clearly that I actually put down my hand of cards and stood up to go upstairs to attend to her. This time the sound was loud. I stood up, walked around the chair and sat down again. I sat down because, yet again, I felt I was only hearing things. The other card players gave me a questioning look and I told them that I thought I had heard something. We got on with the card game and we never said anything more.

The next night was a Tuesday and my wife phoned, as I had been expecting. This was way before the days of mobile phones. After the first few words she told me that she had a little bit of bad news. She told me that our four-year-old daughter had fallen the evening before and had cut the bridge of her nose between and below her eyes. She had hit a low table, I think. This happened, she told me, between half-past eight and nine o'clock.

She also told me that the cut lost so much blood that it was decided to bring her to the nearby hospital. Unusually for a hospital accident department, they got attended to very quickly. A stitch had to be put into the little girl's nose. My wife said the little girl had got very upset during the operation and had cried a lot. When I asked her what time this had happened, my wife told me that everything was over and done with before ten o'clock.

I could not believe the way my wife's story fitted in with my experience the previous night. Around the same time as I heard the cries, my little daughter was in pain and crying from having the stitch right under her eyes. When I told my wife the story, she was just as dumbfounded. At the next game of cards I told the others and, only for the fact that they had remembered me standing up from the table, I don't think they would have believed me.

It's a story I have told many times over the years but I can't say for sure how many occasions it was believed. Some people certainly believe it, especially the older people who have had premonitions or things like that of their own. I don't know whether younger people believe it or not. Some dismiss it. But my wife and I knew from how it matched that it was true.

The same thing has happened every so often, especially with a former school friend of mine. We used to know each other very well when we were very young, but that was a long time ago. We are both now in our 70s. I mightn't think of him for a year. He might suddenly cross my mind and he'd be at the door within an hour. I have gone down to visit him and met him halfway as he was coming to visit me.

Other times I might go over to phone him and the phone would ring and it would be him. I've often phoned him and he would say, 'I was just reaching for the phone, to ring you.' He's the only person this has happened to regularly, maybe ten or fifteen times over the years.

The best example of the lot, concerning that same person, involved a girlfriend he had when he was about 16 or 17. In those days 16 or 17 was a bit young to have a girlfriend. You didn't tell your parents. One night I was standing on the street corner at about a quarter-past-nine and his father walked by. He said, 'Hello.' Having walked by, he then turned back and asked where his son was. Seeing me without him struck him as strange.

Very quickly I said to him, 'I went down home a few minutes ago and when I came back up he had gone missing. He must have gone to one of the shops for something. He'll be back in a minute.' I was lying. I knew he was down the road with the girlfriend. His father walked away and that was it.

I hung around for ages, hoping to intercept my friend, but he went home by a different route. It wasn't until the next day that I met him. He came up to me with a smile on his face and asked me, 'Did you meet my father last night?' I said, 'I did.' He asked me, 'What did you say to him?' I told him the story I had invented.

My friend then said, 'I went in last night and my dad asked me, "Where were you?" I smelled a rat straight away. I said I was with you. My dad asked me, "All night?" I said, "No, we got split up about a quarter-past-nine and I don't know what happened after that."' He had told his father exactly the same story that I had invented, including the same time. It was unbelievable.

I don't have these experiences a lot. They mainly happen with my old school friend and they happened earlier with my daughter. But there are some other examples, including only yesterday when I thought of another lad who I had gone to school with. He is not even a native of where I live. He came down to stay with his grandparents for a while right after the Second World War. Only yesterday I was wondering, 'What happened to him?' Then, last night, I was at the birthday party of one of my daughters and someone said he was asking for me. It was extraordinary.

I don't really know what they are or how to explain them. They are hard to understand. They are hardly premonitions, although there might be elements of a premonition involved in some cases. They more likely involve mental telepathy, especially because the events mostly seem to happen at the one time. Maybe my friend and daughter were so close to me that we were mentally attached. Maybe we knew what the other was doing.

Maybe it's a bit like a man and wife who are so close that they can read each other's thoughts. Perhaps it's a bit like twins who have a strong connection and can know what's going on in each other's minds. But I still don't understand what the reason is in my case. Sometimes you don't want to go into things like this too deeply because you are never sure what you'll find. Ultimately, I suppose, I just don't need to know.

CHARLES, FROM COUNTY ROSCOMMON, can sense things that eventually come to pass.

The strangest one that happened with me dates back to 1963. I worked in London as a stock-keeper at the time. I used to have to go into the office and tell the typist what needed to be ordered. There was one girl there called Carol. She was a small, dark-haired, intelligent girl with glasses. I only knew her as 'Carol'. I never knew her second name. I had no idea of it at all.

One day, one of the lads, who came from Offaly, asked me, 'What's Carol's surname?' I immediately said 'Schneider,' although I hadn't a clue. I don't know where the name came from. It's a strange and unusual name and I never heard it before. It just came into my head.

Although it had just sprung into my head, in the months and years afterwards I kept coming across that name 'Carol Schneider' in newspapers, books and magazines that I bought. I remember buying three different magazines, one after the other, and the name was there.

In 1977, almost 15 years later, I was in a pub in London's Holloway Road. Three girls came in. They were Australian nurses working in London. I was talking to them. One of them looked like Carol from my job years before, although she was a bigger woman.

I remember that we were donating money – £1 each – to a charity and we were signing our names. As I signed my name I looked at the one above it and it was 'Carol Schneider'. That's what she had signed. I had met the girl whose name had entered my head back in 1963! But I never met her again and I never saw that name after that.

What happened struck me as very odd. I can't explain it. The name seemed to become part of my life even though I had never seen it or known it before. It just flashed into my head back in 1963, for some strange reason, and I said it aloud. For 15 years it seemed to stay with me until I eventually met Carol Schneider in 1977. I never heard the name again.

I've had some other experiences like that. When Sonia O'Sullivan was running in the Atlanta Olympics, I knew she would have a bad stomach upset. I just knew she wasn't going to be able to win the 1,500 metres or 5,000 metres because of it. I got this clear-cut picture of what was going to happen about a month or six weeks beforehand.

I was with a group of people who were saying she had a good chance of winning but I said, 'No, she won't.' Everyone thought it was a foregone conclusion that she would win gold but I immediately knew why she wouldn't, that she was going to be violently ill and that she would have to drop out. It just came into my head, as if someone was telling me. I told other people at the time. And that's exactly what happened.

I also predicted when Bernard Dunne was fighting that he would be knocked out in the first round by Kiko Martinez. That fight was a European defence in 2007. I was sitting down and watching a preview on television when it came into my head. He was fighting the following night. I didn't tell anyone about that, unlike what I did with Sonia O'Sullivan. But that's what happened – he was knocked out in the first round.

In all those cases the insights just slip into my mind. I don't know where they come from. I don't know how to explain them. I don't see any images. It's just like something drifting into my mind, like an impulse coming into the brain. And then the things I see tend to happen.

I sometimes wonder if chance could be involved. But I doubt it because, if you take Sonia O'Sullivan, it was a dead cert she was going to win. So I don't know what to think of them. They just happen and I often wonder about them, although they don't bother me at all. Yet I would love to know where they come from and I would like to understand what they are really about.

MARY, FROM COUNTY DOWN, has had a lifelong history of premonitions and telepathic communications.

As I grew up I would have been very close emotionally to my father. There is an intense telepathy between us. As a ten-year-old or eleven-year-old I might be doing my homework in one room and my father would be in the kitchen. I would know what he was thinking. He might be about to come in, to check on my homework. He'd arrive in and say, 'I was just thinking of you.' I'd say, 'I knew you were.'

He even did those psychology tests where he would think 'touch the red pen' or 'lift the green pencil' and I knew exactly what he was saying to me. I didn't even realise what he was doing. I tried it with other people. When I would be at school, I had a friend who sat across at the other side of the class. This was in my first year in grammar school. I could 'think' across to her. It's not that I would tell her answers to things but she would know what I was thinking.

My father was living in Carlow, later on, and I was living in County Down. I remember once getting up and saying, 'I have to go and phone my daddy.' We didn't have a phone where we lived so I had to go down the street to find one. My mother answered the phone. I said, 'Is he OK?' It turned out he was quite ill. He had taken a slight heart attack and had to be brought to hospital. My mother said, 'How did you know?' But, sure, I always know. I don't see that as amazing.

I also knew when my granny was going to die. She died when I was 16. I knew that she was going to go. My daddy was with her in Kerry, where she lived, and I was in County Down. We were due to go to mass. I remember turning to my mother and saying, 'I can't go to ten o'clock mass. I'll wait until 11 o'clock. Daddy is going to ring.' My mother said, 'What do you mean?' I said, 'Because Nana has died!' My mother said, 'What?' My daddy did ring and my granny had died. I had known that she was gone.

On the morning when my granny's sister died in Donegal, I woke up and I knew that she had passed away. I had an awareness of her being in my house. I think she came to me and said goodbye. It's not that I saw a ghost or anything like that. It was just a sort of sense that she was gone. It's like a 'knowing'. It's not creepy or anything. It's a peaceful feeling. In those last two situations, in particular, it was a nice feeling to know that they were at peace.

Another morning I got up and knew I had to get everything tidied up in the house. I felt something was about to happen. It was like I was waiting for a phone call, all day, knowing that someone was going to ring me. They did. It turned out that my husband's father had collapsed and taken a stroke. That's how I heard the bad news.

I also never like stormy nights. Some years ago, on a wild, stormy and wet night, a girl who was a friend of my daughter's was celebrating her birthday. All the girls decided to go out. I asked my daughter, 'Do you have to go out tonight?' She said, 'It's her birthday.'

So she went and I went to bed. But, at one o'clock, I turned to my husband and I said, 'You need to go out and find our daughter!' He said, 'Why?' I said, 'You just need to go down and get her and bring her home!'

I had a very bad feeling. I knew that something was going to happen. So my husband reluctantly got out of bed and went down to get her. He found her with two friends and said, 'It's a bad night. Hop in. I'll take you all home.'

The other girl, whose birthday it was, went on to a party and she died tragically from shock as a result of an allergy. I knew something was coming and I just wanted my daughter safely home.

I also had a nephew who died. He was two-and-a-half at the time and my eldest daughter was three. He was coming from England on holiday to my granny's. One night, some days before it happened, I remember coming down the stairs and sitting on the bottom step. I turned to my husband and I said, 'I have to take our daughter and go to my mum's and see

75

my mum and my granny.' My husband said, 'But aren't the others coming?' I felt something was going to happen to my mum's mum, who was quite old at the time.

I had a strong feeling that I had to take my daughter with me. So off we went. We went by train, the next morning, to Dublin and on to Carlow. On the morning we were travelling home, we got up and we were excited at the thought of coming back.

The other family were due to arrive from England around lunchtime. Because of that I said we wouldn't rush. Instead of getting the nine o'clock train we got the one about twelve o'clock. I went to the corner shop to get a bar of chocolate and a drink for the little girl before leaving.

When I came out of the shop I saw my mother coming in the door against me. She said, 'There has been an accident!' I knew immediately it was a death. I thought it was my granny. But my mother said that my nephew had been drowned on the farm.

I immediately knew that my daughter would have been with him if I hadn't taken her away, because they would have been playing together. I didn't see exactly what was going to happen but I knew I had to take my daughter to somewhere safe.

On the morning of 9/11 I also had a forewarning. I had a very visual image in a dream. I dreamt of an accountant who was an acquaintance. When I woke up I said to my husband, 'I was in a building, overlooking a river, and it's all accountants. It's the morning after the night before and they've all come in happy to work.'

I thought my dream had something to do with accountants. I also felt I had been in this building experiencing what people went through before they died. I just knew it was all connected to accountants. That's what kept coming to me. I got news, later on, of what had happened. I found out that a lot of accountants who worked in the Twin Towers had died.

To me all these things are either a sense of awareness or a premonition. They are a part of life with me. They happen all the time. It's not that I think about them. It's just that I've had them all my life. My granny also had them and my daddy has them as well. I count it as a blessing.

Some people think it's creepy but it's a part of me. I think that people who have lived on the land are aware of it. They look at the weather and the patterns of the water. Maybe it's some ability that we have always had, that we used years ago.

I am also Catholic and my parents would have had great devotion. It's more of a faith than a practising Catholicism. So I would very much have a sense of the cycle of life and a sense of life being a continuum.

Many people, as a child, believe, 'Oh, my God! I'm going to grow up and die!' But I never had that. I always had a sense that you'll go to a place of peace. I believe that from before you are born to after you die you are with those you love. Those you have loved walk with you, every day, and never go away.

I also know I am sensitive. Years ago I was diagnosed with a previously-undiagnosed heart condition. I was one of those people who were never supposed to have lived. Medically they don't understand how I survived.

Maybe that has something to do with it. Maybe I was meant to be here. Whatever it is I am certainly aware of things that are going to happen and they often bring me a great sense of peace. It's just who I am.

HENRY LAW, FROM COUNTY DERRY, is an identical twin of his brother Dick. They are both in their 40s. Their story illustrates the sense of telepathy, closeness and common understanding – not to mention forewarning-like sensations – that can exist between twins. Their experiences, to some extent, are similar to what you have just read about in the previous case history.

My brother Dick and I were born within minutes of each other and we grew up very close. We are identical. People confuse us all the time. We are both unmarried, with no offspring. We chose the same sort of work environments, although in different places. We have the same taste in animals – we don't like dogs; we prefer cats. We also have the same choice and colour of car.

If he is down in the dumps, I am down in the dumps. If he's tired, I'm tired. When he's awake, I'm awake. Whenever I start to yawn, I know he's tired and he's yawning too. He once had a leg injury, on his left knee. When his got swollen, mine got swollen with it – and I never had a leg injury. Mine also hurt where his hurt.

We also tend to have the same tastes. When it comes to renting films, for example, I don't have to phone home and ask him if he wants to see the one I'm about to choose. I just know he wants to watch it too. We even have the same teeth crowned in the same places in our mouths. Our dentist says, 'In the event of a plane crash, heaven knows how we could identify one from the other.'

We have younger brothers, Brian and Keith, who are twins too. They don't have the same looks but similar things happen. One had to have his appendix out; two weeks later his twin brother had to have his out as well. They had the same symptoms and the same complaints. It's very creepy that way.

Every member of my staff at work has confused Dick for me. He could come in and do my work and no one would notice. He could drive in, park in my spot and wear my uniform. I could tell him where to go and what to do and no one would be any the wiser. I could probably do the same at his place.

There are some differences. We both grew up in the 80s and his preference in music is heavy rock, like AC/DC and Black Sabbath, whereas mine is Status Quo. I suppose, though, while both of those choices are different they are also alike. We also have different tastes in TV. He loves cookery programmes, whereas I can't stand that stuff.

Dick would be more for going into pubs, whereas I would prefer a quiet or outdoor life. Dick also stands on the left side of a photograph, as you look at it. We do it all the time. But that's because we line up alphabetically, with Dick on the left and me, Henry, on the right.

There's another difference too. Dick was born first so his face is a little bit longer and narrower. Mine is rounder. In the last four weeks of a normal pregnancy, the first baby is lying in the birth canal surrounded by the mother's organs and the weight of the next baby lying on top of him. The result is that his skull takes a narrower shape. The one up above is more able to move around so he will have a rounder face. That's exactly the case with us.

Despite these differences we are always confused for each other. Some years ago, for example, both of us were giving blood. We happened to go to the same place. My brother came in first and then I arrived. When I went in my brother was finished. He was getting his tea or coffee. The nurse said to me, 'I've just taken blood from you.' I had to say to her, 'Look over there. That's my brother.' I didn't get to see her expression because I was just after lying down. But I presume it scared the life out of her. It always does.

Another event happened during the Troubles, when the British Army were here. Dick was driving one car and I was driving another car. He was two cars ahead of me so he came to a checkpoint first. He was stopped by the soldier. The soldier took his details and away Dick went. The next car was waved on. Then I was stopped. I rolled down the window and the soldier immediately said, 'How did you do that? You were just in that car in front.' I explained to him but he couldn't get inside his head that we were twins.

I also know what Dick is thinking. I remember, way back in school, a teacher once asked my twin brother to go into a room and write something down. He was told what to write. I think the word was 'pair', as in pair of people. I was then asked to come in and write down what I thought he had written. The only thing was that our spelling wasn't up to scratch and I wrote down 'pear', as in fruit. But it was close. The teacher said to the rest of the class, 'How do you explain that?' I always remember that.

If I let my mind go blank, right now, I will know exactly what he's doing. I will know if he's at home watching TV. I will have a feeling that he's sitting down and relaxing. If we are standing in the same room, we can make the same food choices for each other. I know exactly what he's going to order. If we go into a restaurant and look at the menus, he'll know what I'm looking for and I'll know what he's looking for. It's just a feeling that you get.

We were both recently going to a family gathering. He asked me, 'What about the two of us wearing the same clothes?' I said, 'No, I don't want to.' He said, 'That's OK. I knew you were going to say that.' He actually did know what I would think but he was just running it past me anyway. He knew what I was going to say but he just wanted to hear it for himself. He did, mind you, ask me again and by then I had changed my mind. So he eventually got his way. He must have known I would eventually say, 'Yes.'

I suppose you could say there is telepathy between us. We've always shared the same thoughts. You could say that, in the case of twins, the closer they are in terms of looks and behaviour they will share a lot more thoughts. Years ago if I needed to find Dick I could find him that way. However, nowadays, because of mobile technology you just lift the phone and you find him. You don't need to use that side of your mind so much.

The truth is that we always have had this, on a daily basis, so we don't think about it much. We never think, 'God! That was weird!' We just carry on. It just happens. I suppose you never miss a well until the water runs dry. It's only if something very weird happens that we might find it fascinating. Otherwise it's just commonplace. And it's not something I've experienced with my other friends or companions – it's only with Dick.

There's only one thing I have regretted over the years. We almost had different birthdays. Dick was born at 11.49 p.m. I was born at 11.59 p.m. A minute later and we would have been identical twins but born on different days.

We would have loved that as kids. There was nothing we hated more than sharing the same cake and blowing out the candles together. We sort of felt cheated. Wouldn't it have been great? That would have been exceptionally different, wouldn't it?

EILEEN, FROM COUNTY LOUTH, was overcome by a sudden, strange feeling that her uncle was going to die. It happened in early 2011.

I had an uncle who lived in Donegal. He was severely autistic. He lost his speech when he was young. I always used to go visit him and I always wanted to see him. I liked 'special children'.

We all grew up being told, 'He's not going to see 21. He's going to die.' He was taking seizures and we were always being warned, 'This is it!' But he reached 50 and not a thing had happened to him.

Then, one day, in March 2011, I was travelling down the road in a car. My partner was driving. The sky looked very grey. I started thinking of my uncle and this awful feeling came over me.

It was a strange feeling, like my uncle was telling me, 'I've had enough!' The feeling wasn't so much that *he* had had enough; it was more that his *body* had had enough. It was as if his voice was saying it to me. Yet he didn't have a voice as he had not been able to speak.

The feeling I was getting was that my uncle couldn't take any more, that he couldn't go on. There was a sort of greyness about how I felt. I felt very sad and wanted to go and visit him.

I said it to my partner that I had this urge to see him. However, as I was coming in the road afterwards, I was a bit worried about what had happened and I was thinking, 'I hope I don't get this sort of feeling again at night. I hope this is all there's going to be. I hope this is it.'

About two weeks later I got a phone call telling me that my uncle had been taken to Letterkenny Hospital. One of his lungs was badly congested. They tried everything, including a ventilator and different things. They couldn't get him to eat. He eventually died. He was only in his 50s.

Unfortunately I hadn't gone to visit him before he died. It was all too late by the time I heard. But I really did want to be with him. I would have liked to have sat with him for a night. I ended up, instead, going to Donegal for the funeral.

What happened didn't frighten me and I don't really care who dismisses it. We all knew my uncle wasn't in the best of health but it had gone on for so long. He had been having seizures since he was young, yet he had always bounced back and survived all the seizures and pneumonia.

He'd always revive, his heart was so strong. So there was no reason for what I thought in the car to come into my mind at that time. It was most strange. It was most unusual. I suppose it was a premonition. What else could it have been?

DONNA, WHO COMES ORIGINALLY FROM COUNTY TYRONE but who now lives in County Derry, had a forewarning of an accident involving two of her children. Although the warning came in the form of a message, it also generated a 'feeling' that something bad was about to occur. The event happened in the early 2000s.

I went to bed, one night, and fell asleep. There was absolutely nothing on my mind. I quickly started tossing and turning. I kept hearing my name, 'Donna! Donna! Donna! Donna!' It was in my head. It was a female voice and it went on over a long period of time. I kept waking up and wondering, 'What is wrong?' The first time I looked at the clock it was ten-minutes-to-five in the morning.

When I woke up I felt, 'That must have been the worst night's sleep I ever had.' I said to my husband, 'There's going to be a bad accident today and somebody is going to die!' He said, 'Don't be ridiculous.' I said, 'I'm serious. The whole night I heard a voice calling my name. I don't know why but it makes me think somebody is going to die, there's going to be a bad accident.' I can't explain why I had this feeling. I never had it before and I never had it since.

My husband tried to reassure me. He said, 'You were probably lost in your sleep and somebody was calling your name.' He was sort of joking about it. But it was a really dark feeling and I felt so bad that I phoned my dad and my three brothers to make sure they were OK. I was asking them, 'How are things?' I wanted to check that they were fine. It turned out that they were.

Later that day my husband and I had an argument. I left the house and went to a friend of ours. I left at about three o'clock in the afternoon. Our two eldest were playing over in a neighbour's house, where they had children of the same age. Our youngest was still at home. I heard later that, as soon as I left, the youngest child fell and split his eye on the coffee-table. He was only two years of age. He had been running about and fell.

My husband decided to take him to the hospital, to see if he needed stitches. As they were heading down the road, there was a police cordon diverting the traffic. My husband took a different road and went to the hospital. When he arrived, he went in and our neighbour was there. The neighbour said, 'How did you find out?' My husband said, 'What do you mean? I'm here because our youngest fell and cut his eye.'

The neighbour then told my husband that our other two children had been involved in a car accident. My husband was shocked. He was even more upset when he heard one of the doctors saying, 'The ambulance is on its way and there is one fatality.' He didn't know, at that stage, who it was that was dead.

What had happened was that our neighbours had decided

to go for a chicken dinner. They took the children along with them. They were eventually coming back home. A fellow living nearby had a motorbike, which he had just bought and fixed, and he took it out on the road to check it. He went out without his helmet. He was on a country road, like a laneway, that led up to the main road where our neighbour's car was driving along. His brakes failed and he went straight into the side of the car.

My neighbour's car ended up upside down in a field. The motorcyclist was killed. Our two children had glass splinters to the face and they were brought by ambulance to the hospital while our neighbours went on ahead. They were also very shocked.

Our oldest boy still talks about it and he can remember the motorcyclist's head hitting off the back passenger-seat window. We were just as shocked, later on, when we discovered that the accident had happened at ten-minutes-to-five in the afternoon, the same time as I had looked at the clock in the morning.

I believe that my mother, who had passed away about six months before, was sending me a message. I already had a strange experience involving her, which happened directly after she died. She died aged 56 from breast cancer. Shortly after her death a friend's wife suggested to me that I should ask for my mum to send me a message telling me if she is happy where she is. I thought, 'You must be off your head.' She said, 'You must ask for something that you don't think you are going to get anyway.'

I couldn't get what she said out of my head. So I came up with something. I said, 'Right, Mummy, when you are happy I want you to get Dad to give me a bouquet of flowers.' My dad had never bought me flowers in my life. He would always give presents but never flowers.

Soon after that my dad phoned me and said, 'I don't know what to get your granny for Christmas. I was thinking of getting her flowers.' I said, 'That's a good idea.' He also said he would get flowers for the partners of two of my brothers. I said, 'That's perfect.'

I was thinking, 'God! If only you had got me a bouquet of flowers, I would have been so happy.' Anyhow, just before Christmas I called into my dad. I asked him if he wanted anything in the shops and he said he didn't. He then said, 'There's a bouquet of flowers out in the kitchen for you.' I couldn't believe it. I was amazed. I said, 'Why did you do that?' He said, 'I only ordered three bouquets in the florist's but when I went to pick them up they had made me four.'

I told him, 'You are not going to believe me but I asked Mummy to get you to give me a bouquet of flowers if she is happy where she is.' All he said was, 'I can tell you I did not order you a bouquet of flowers.' I wondered, 'Who did?' I cried the whole way home. I dried the flowers and still have them, even though I really don't believe in that sort of stuff and I'm a complete sceptic.

I feel that my mother is around and I think, regarding the accident, that she was warning me there was something coming. Yet I often wonder, 'If it really was a sign from my mother, how could she still let it happen because she loved me so much?' It also definitely wasn't my mum's voice that I heard while asleep.

But I still ask, 'How did I know something was coming? How did I know there was going to be an accident? How did it happen at exactly the same time as the time that morning when I opened my eyes and looked at the clock?'

I also believe I have a sixth sense, a certain ability to know that something is happening that shouldn't be happening. I can usually pinpoint it very quickly. It probably goes back to my later teens. I can spot white lies. I never know if it is coincidence or what. I believe I have this ability but I question it on the other hand. Yet I know that what happened that day of the accident did happen. I definitely believe I was given a sign.

JONATHAN, FROM COUNTY KILDARE, who we heard from earlier, also had a forewarning of his grandfather's death.

I was in my friend's house one day. There was a group of us there, in the sitting-room. I remember *The Simpsons* was on in the background. All of a sudden, just for a split second, I got this feeling that there was bad news coming. I also knew it was going to be about my grandfather.

Suddenly my mobile phone rang. As it rang I said, 'It's something to do with Granddad! It's something bad!' It came from nowhere. I had this strong feeling that what I was going to hear was awful and I knew what it was going to be about.

It was my mother and she said, 'I've got bad news. Your granddad, in Wexford, is after dying.' I couldn't believe it, although I knew at the same time. I wasn't shocked. I sensed before she spoke what she was going to say. She told me that my dad was already on his way to Wexford, straight from work, and the rest of us were going to go down in the next few hours.

The strange thing was that there was nothing wrong with Granddad at the time. He wasn't in hospital or he wasn't sick. He had died of a sudden heart attack which no one could have seen coming. Also, when I'd get a phone call around that time of day, it would usually be my mother saying, 'Your dinner is ready. Come home.' For some reason, though, I definitely knew that this was going to be different.

The feeling came to me so quickly. It was a sinking, dark feeling that what I was going to hear would be bad. It was strange, like a warning that something was happening. I didn't say it to my mother at the time. I told her a couple of months afterwards. I said, 'I knew before the phone rang that I was going to hear about Granddad.' She thought it was strange. She said, 'How could you have known?'

This sort of thing doesn't happen to me a lot, although I am the sort of person who sometimes gets a gut feeling about different things. I get it about people, in particular. But I don't get it all the time. I think it might be something in me. My mother is like that also. She'd get a bad feeling about things as well. My dad, on the other hand, doesn't get them at all.

I think other people get them too. Certain people are like that, they just get what's like a bad sensation deep down in their stomach, in their gut. I'm sure, just like with me, it gives them a slight satisfaction that they are able to know what is going to happen before it takes place. A lot of people would say, 'It's just coincidence.' But I think it's more than that. They are definitely warnings of things to come.

FRANK, FROM COUNTY TYRONE, had a feeling that he was going to become ill. It happened in the mid-1990s.

I was working in London at the time. I was in my early 40s and in good health. My work, however, was stressful and every evening I'd be shattered when I'd get home. The work was very methodical. I started work early, at eight o'clock, and I worked hard. But I swam a lot and did mountain-walking as well.

One morning I was in the office, sitting at my desk. It was in early spring, around February or March. It was just a normal day, somewhere between nine and eleven o'clock. I think I was taking a breather and sat back in my chair. I suddenly got this feeling that something was going to happen to me. What I felt was very uncomfortable. It was like a shivery, cold sensation that went through my whole body.

I definitely thought something was going to happen. It was more bad than good. It wasn't that the feeling was like, 'I'm going to die tomorrow.' There was no time-period connected to it. But it was very noticeable and I thought it might have been cancer. The feeling didn't last very long, maybe only seconds. It then disappeared and I got on with my work. I didn't say it to anyone.

A short time afterwards I left my job and I joined a bigger company. I had been offered more money. I was only with the new company for six weeks when I was made redundant. This was at the end of April. I remember well the Friday evening when it happened. At the time I didn't make any connection with the feeling I had a few months before.

I then decided to go on a teacher training course. I applied to a college in the North of England and I was accepted. I had a few months off and I started the course the following autumn. We used to have to do periods of practical teaching out in colleges and I found that stressful. Any time I had to do it, I never slept the night before. Everything was new to me. By Christmastime I had lost a lot of sleep.

I got a very bad cold or flu that Christmas. It went for me straight away. I got it one day and by the next day it had really attacked me. I had a terrible cough and I couldn't get rid of it. The net result was that I felt bad when I started back at the course after Christmas. I kept swimming in the hope it might help me get rid of the cold, but it didn't work.

Instead things got worse and I lost the power of my right leg. I had been trailing the leg for some time before that but I thought I had pulled a muscle or something at my swimming. It was getting so bad that one of the students said, 'You had better go and see somebody about it.' So I went to a doctor, who was attached to the college, and he diagnosed that my sciatic nerve was inflamed.

Then someone said, 'Go to a physiotherapist.' So I went to one and she checked me over. She then said, 'Before I can treat you I have to send you to your doctor, to check out your neurology.' These were all new terms to me. The doctor got me into hospital straight away and I was told I had lesions on my spinal cord and my brain. There are sheaths around the nerves and they were damaged.

I struggled on and got my teaching qualification and went back down to London. My body seemed to give up. It got really bad. About six months later I was diagnosed with ME syndrome or chronic fatigue. I've had it ever since. The continuing symptoms have been weakness, tiredness and exhaustion. My leg is very weak. I haven't been able to work in an office since, although I can work from home.

I can't quite remember when exactly I connected what I felt in the office with my subsequent illness. But I did make the connection and the word I used is that I had a 'premonition'. The premonition might have been that *something* was going to happen, although I would suspect it was directly to do with the illness and not just about being made redundant as you can always go out and get another job. The ME was different – it changed my life.

I did have another premonition, once before, so I know what they are about. I was brought up on a farm and I used to drive the tractor and bale hay. I was only about 15, 16 or 17 at the time. Someone loaned us a tractor and the very next day I was going to be doing a lot of work. That was brilliant for me, to be doing all that driving. A great day was lined up. You couldn't get better.

The night beforehand, when I went off to bed, I had an uncomfortable feeling that things were not going to go right the next day. And that's what happened. The next day the baler kept breaking down and the whole day was destroyed. I had an uncomfortable feeling that it wasn't going to work out and it didn't. That was devastating to a young teenager like me, who wanted to do a lot of driving on a tractor.

So I think having premonitions is possible, especially if you are quite well developed in that area. But I wasn't into any therapies or 'higher-self' at the time and had no awareness of these things. All I had was just an uncomfortable feeling that something was going to go wrong with the baler and, later on, with me. Both feelings were very uncomfortable and maybe something, or somebody, from a higher level was getting in touch to warn me.

I sometimes wonder, regarding my illness, if something was already happening to me. Was I tired or something and my body noticed it? Illnesses don't just happen today – they might start a year beforehand and materialise later. So maybe I was tuning in to something at a subconscious or unconscious level.

I certainly had a feeling, either way, that something was going to happen to me and it did. And I've always said to people, 'I had a premonition.' I have always used that word, that I had a 'premonition' that I was going to become unwell.

SINÉAD, FROM COUNTY GALWAY, has had premonitions of many future events. They started in her early teens and have continued ever since.

The first experience I had was about five days before my grandmother died. I was only 14 at the time. This was on a Sunday. We came down to her house to see her. She wasn't sick or anything; we just came to visit. As we were leaving – as I was saying goodbye to her – I just knew in my head that it would be the last time that I'd see her.

She gave me a hug when I was leaving. Something in my

head told me to take a good look at her and to remember what she was like. I looked at her earrings and saw what she was wearing. I wanted to remember these things about her because I knew I wouldn't see her again.

I was going to say it to someone but I felt they would have thought I was mad. I also worried that it might have been some weird notion I had. I kind of forgot about it then. The following Thursday they found her dead, reading the newspaper in her house. I thought, 'Oh, God! I knew that would happen!'

Another event happened a few years ago. I was at home, in the living-room, dozing off on the couch. It was the middle of the day. I wasn't really asleep and what I had wasn't really a dream. I just got this thing into my head, like a message. It was like a voice. It mentioned a person's first name and it said that he would 'die tomorrow, Saturday.' Although it mentioned the name, I couldn't figure out who it was.

At the time I had a friend who was going out with a fellow who had the same first name. I thought it was him that this was about. I went, 'Oh, my God!' I texted my friend and said it to her. I told her what had happened. She said, 'What's wrong with you? Don't be saying things like that.' I said, 'I'm just telling you what happened. I'm just telling you that this has happened with me before, but maybe it's not him.'

The following day I got a phone call from my mum. She told me that a cousin of mine had died in a car accident. He had the same name and was just 30 years of age. I hadn't even thought about him. It seems he was just driving along and he crashed the car into a ditch. He was epileptic and they reckoned he might have had a fit. I rang my friend and said, 'Don't worry. It's not your boyfriend.'

I was worried especially because of what had happened before with my granny. I really believed that this was going to take place and that the person would die. I also continued to have experiences like this and they have lasted for about six years so far. They have always happened when something big would occur, like a death. I never think, 'Oh, a red car is going to pass me now' and it would happen. It would never be something small.

I had another one when my baby was born. The whole time I was pregnant I knew I would have a boy and I did. I also knew I would have him early, which happened again. But I knew, as well, that there would be something wrong with the baby, that he wouldn't have 100 per cent health. He was born with a metabolic condition. Thankfully it wasn't anything more serious. It is manageable.

I kept saying to them, when they were taking scans, 'Are you sure everything is OK?' But there was no way they could have told with scans and it wasn't in our family. It was only when he was born and had a screening-test that they knew there was something wrong. Then I said, 'Oh! So that's it! That's what was wrong!' I knew all along. It was always in the back of my head and I said it a few times to people.

I did have a good premonition once. A friend of mine was expecting a baby. She never knew if it would be a boy or a girl. I went to bed, one night, and had a dream that she had a baby boy and he was a fine ten-pound boy. He was a big, bouncing boy and I was going to visit him. His weight really stuck in my head.

The next morning I texted around and asked people if they had heard anything. I mentioned about my dream and that in it she had a big baby boy. But no one had heard anything at that stage. That night I got a text that she had her baby and it was a nine-pound-ten-ounce boy.

I don't really know what it is that goes on. My mam always says that I am intuitive, that I read people really well.

She said that, when I was younger, I was always like that with people. If someone was sad, for example, I'd know it without them saying it. But I don't call myself psychic or anything like that. I just don't know what it is.

I know a lot of people don't believe in these sorts of things, but I do. If someone said to me that they had a feeling about something, I'd believe them because I know what it's like. But it can be hard. When my cousin died I was worried. You are kind of carrying that with you. You don't know if you should tell someone or if there's anything you can do about it.

I ask myself, 'Should I maybe try to stop the thing from happening?' But you can't just ring people and tell them that someone is going to die tomorrow. You don't want to be scaring people and you might be wrong. And there's really nothing that can be done. I think, at the end of the day, if it's going to happen it's going to happen. You might know early but there's probably nothing you can do about it. You can't stop destiny, I think.

PREDICTIVE DREAMS

In 1858 the American author Mark Twain had a most vivid and disturbing dream. He was, at the time, in his early 20s and employed as a steersman on the Mississippi riverboat *Pennsylvania*. His brother Henry, who was two years his junior, worked as a mud clerk on the same packet steamer. Twain's dream concerned Henry and, much more worryingly, his death.

In the dream Henry was laid out like a corpse. He lay in a metallic coffin and was dressed in his brother's suit. On his breast was a large bouquet of flowers, consisting mainly of white roses but with a red rose in the centre. 'The dream was so vivid, so like reality, that it deceived me, and I thought it was real,' Twain – whose real name was Samuel Langhorne Clemens – remarked.

Twain was further concerned that, on the night of the dream, Henry's goodbyes to the family had been somewhat strange. He had, as usual, said his farewell in the second-floor sitting-room of the family's residence and then proceeded downstairs to leave. This time, however, their mother, who was moved by something in Henry's manner, had gone to the top of the stairs and said goodbye again. Not only that but Henry had rushed back upstairs and bade farewell once more.

Some weeks afterwards the *Pennsylvania* sailed from New Orleans with Henry on board but without Mark Twain, who had a row with one of the boat's pilots and had asked to be left ashore. So worried was Twain, however, that on the night before the boat's departure he advised his brother on how to save himself in the event of a disaster. Twain's concern proved to be extraordinarily predictive as, a few days later, the boat's boilers exploded at Ship Island, below Memphis. Henry was injured in the tragedy.

Twain hastened to the scene and located his brother, who soon passed away. Although the coffins provided for those who had died were of cheap unpainted pine, the ladies of Memphis had clubbed together and bought a metallic case which Henry's body reposed in. The suit Henry was laid out in had once belonged to his brother. 'I recognised instantly that my dream of several weeks before was here exactly reproduced,' Mark Twain concluded.

However, there was still one thing missing – the bouquet of flowers. At exactly the same moment that the future author became conscious of this, an elderly lady entered the room and placed a large bouquet of flowers on his brother's breast. It consisted mainly of white roses with a red rose prominently displayed right in the centre. Mark Twain's dream had come to fruition.

What Mark Twain had experienced through his dream, back in 1858, was a classic case of precognitive or predictive dreaming. His subconscious mind, during sleep, had perceived a future event that had eventually come to pass. It might reasonably be said that the scene he dreamt of could not have been deduced from the senses or from information available at the time it occurred. Putting it quite simply, he had future sight.

Predictive dreams that occur during sleep are remarkably common. So also are waking dreams or waking images. These are the often short, sharp pictures or dreamlike thoughts that spontaneously intrude on the mind while a person is awake. Sometimes the images are referred to as 'flashes.' They often, although not exclusively, occur when a person is tired, bored, distracted or relaxed. Both categories – sleep dreams and waking images – are featured in this chapter.

ELIZABETH, WHO LIVES IN COUNTY CLARE, was forewarned of her brother's death.

I was living abroad after college, back in the late 1970s. I spent two years working there on a project. When I was getting ready to come back, I had a dream of my brother. In my dream he was driving a car. He drove the car down the hill towards the house that my family were living in. He lost control of the car and smashed into the house. There was devastation. Everything was destroyed and everything was chaos. My brother, above all, seemed so vulnerable in the dream.

I had the dream only once but it disturbed me an awful lot. Shortly afterwards I returned home. I got back around Christmas. From the minute I got home I knew that death was coming to our house. It was like some sort of darkness overhung everything. My brother was very troubled and was in a terrible state. He had come back to live at home and was very introverted. He was isolating himself and there was a lot of trauma. It was a very upsetting time.

I was devastated by what was happening. My brother, just like in my dream, was very vulnerable. I sometimes wondered about my family, 'Why don't they know what's coming?' The months passed by and the chaos remained. I remember, one day, I was wearing black clothes and somebody said, 'You look like you are going to a funeral.' I was thinking, 'Don't say that! I am!' I knew death was coming, although I didn't know it was going to be my brother. I just knew something terrible was going to happen.

One day I was attending a wedding. When I arrived at the

wedding place, I knew that something was wrong. I remember saying that at the time. I left the wedding early and went to the train station. When I got there, for some reason, I was one of the few people who weren't going to be able to get on the train. I was almost hysterical, saying, 'You have to get me on the train.' They said, 'It's OK! We'll let you on.' I sat on the train and I cried the whole way home.

When I got home my mother was pacing the house. My brother was late home. The rest of the family were saying, 'It's OK! He's always late for mealtime. Don't be so worried.' But my mother was agitated. She was in a bad way. I know that she had experienced forewarnings before. When things had gone badly for me in the past, and I hadn't told anyone, she had known that something was wrong.

I left to meet someone and was cycling into the town. As I was cycling away from my home, the wind blew something off my bicycle. I had this distinct feeling that I should go no further, that it was like some sort of message that I should go back. It was only five minutes back to the house. So I turned about. When I got home the police were there.

What had happened was that my brother had gone out for a swim and he had drowned. We learned later that he had been calling for help but no one could reach him on time. I think the dream was some sort of forewarning to prepare me for what was going to occur. I knew something was coming and it did happen. I think people are susceptible to the energies that are there and that pass between us. We all have this ability but some people have thinner veils than others.

I believe that when something really profound is coming towards you, you get messages. I think that your life is known beforehand and some people have foreknowledge all the way along. Time doesn't seem to have the significance that we give to it. It's not linear. I feel I had a forewarning. I know I did.

MAIRÉAD, FROM COUNTY CORK, had a chilling dream of being violently assaulted. It came to her one Sunday night back in May 2010.

I was living with my partner in England at the time. It was my first serious relationship after my marriage had broken up. We had gone to bed, as we usually did, quite early. I eventually fell asleep. The dream I had was very vivid. I could see myself in the dream and my skin looked absolutely perfect, without blemish and flawless. I looked perfectly healthy. My hair was flowing and I was standing up.

I then saw what looked like 12 knuckles around my neck. It was a bit like two hands tightly wrapped around the neck area, with the fingers like rings. It seemed like I had a huge ring-chain all the way around and it was tight. I couldn't make out whether they were male knuckles or not.

All this time my eyes were open. Everything was so vivid that I could see my eyelashes. I could see sky and clouds behind me. I then saw my skin going whitish. I realised that I couldn't breathe and my skin started to go slightly grey. My skin then began to go indigo. But, all this time, there was little expression on my face. There was no emotion whatsoever. There was no panic.

All I knew was that I couldn't breathe. No part of my body could move. I was totally limp, as if my whole body was dead. I then had this knowingness, 'You can't breathe, so just surrender, it's OK!' When I surrendered I woke up and I felt, 'That was a strange dream.' But there was still no emotion whatsoever. It wasn't like a nightmare or anything. I was completely dissociated. It was about half-two or three o'clock, so I went back to sleep again.

After breakfast, the following morning, I rang one of my best friends in Cork. I told her, 'I had the strangest dream last night.' The two of us must have spent an hour-and-a-half discussing it. There was no reason for it that I could think of. I was in a good place at the time. Everything was fine. Although my partner had a short fuse, he had never touched me. I didn't wake up with the quilt tucked around me or an arm around my neck, or anything like that.

My friend and I went through the dream. We both thought that it was symbolic and significant. I knew it was important. We talked about whether there was something wrong about my communication and it wanted to come out. Was I being guided in some way? Was it a warning? Perhaps I wasn't as healthy as I should be? We had this really big conversation and then it was over with. I forgot about the dream and moved on.

One week later, to the day, my partner and I had been out. We had got an Indian take-away and brought it home. It was about half-seven in the evening. We had an argument and, whatever I said, he just flipped. It wasn't our usual type of argument. All I can remember, within seconds, was his face in front of mine.

The next thing I recall was that his hands were around my throat. I couldn't breathe and my whole body was limp. I couldn't even struggle because of whatever way he caught me. I could see his eyes looking straight into mine. I remember trying to beg with my eyes, to get him to stop. That was the only tool I had. The thing from my dream then came to me, 'Surrender! It's OK!'

We were in the kitchen, where there was a big window, and just like in my dream I could see clouds outside. There was almost a feeling of peace. It's not like my heart was even pounding. There was this knowingness that it would be OK. But when he didn't stop I felt, 'This is my last breath!' I then just floated outside of myself, although I wasn't looking down on myself or anything like that.

I woke up on the ground. I must have gone unconscious for quite some time. I must have been out for an hour-and-a-half. There was blood all around me. It was like a pool of blood and, at that point, I had no idea where it came from. I was mesmerised. All I did was go across the floor, grab the phone and dial 999. They asked me what had happened and if my partner was still there. I remember saying, 'I don't know.'

My partner had actually gone upstairs, although I didn't know it at the time. I locked myself in another bedroom and lay on the bed. A short time later the police and an ambulance arrived. They took my partner away and, from what I heard afterwards, he said he had flipped and completely lost it. He said he didn't know what came over him and he didn't know that he had it in him.

I was taken to hospital, where they treated my wounds. I remember waking up there the following morning. My face was encrusted with blood and I felt I was glued to the pillow. But I was in an incredibly peaceful place. All I knew was that I had to go back to Ireland. It wasn't a panic thing. I knew something had shifted and I had to go home. It was as clear as day to me. I remember saying to one of the nurses, 'I'm ready.'

I definitely saw the event before it happened, although I didn't see who was behind it. I think I got a forewarning of something that was going to happen, that it was going to be OK and that I would then understand a bigger picture. It's almost as if this drastic thing had to happen to bring this about. I had been ignoring all the signs. There was a bigger picture there and that was to return to Ireland. So I came home shortly afterwards.

I think our subconscious knows everything that is going on. Our subconscious can pick up on other energies. If you walk into a room, you can pick up the energy. You know who to avoid. I don't even like using the word subconscious because 'sub' makes it sound like it is underneath. It is more our spirit. I think everything is stored inside, like in a filing cabinet. And I thoroughly believe that, in my case, it's like one file was pulled out and put right in my face on that Sunday back in May 2010.

HELEN, FROM COUNTY WESTMEATH, dreamt of her friend's father's heart attack. It happened back in the 1980s.

I was about 20 years old at the time and I was working in Dublin. I came home one Friday night, as I did every weekend. I went to bed as usual. That first night home I had a bad dream. It was very vivid and multicoloured and I felt I was there watching what was going on. The dream was about my friend's father, who I hadn't seen in about a fortnight. I dreamt he had a heart attack.

I could see my friend in the back of the ambulance with her father. It wasn't her mother or her sister in the ambulance, it was her. You would normally expect it to have been the wife. My friend was strapped in with a seatbelt and she was very agitated and very upset. The paramedics were working on her father. I could actually see them bending over, trying to restart his heart.

I woke up in the morning and my mother came into the room, bringing me a cup of tea. I explained to her the whole thing in detail. I told my mother specifically that it was my friend who was in the ambulance. And I told her about my friend's father's heart attack. My mother said, 'Oh, that's terrible! I saw him the other day and he was in great health.'

I then thought no more about it until that afternoon when I bumped into my friend's sister down the town. She came over to me in the street and stopped me to tell me that her dad had experienced a heart attack in the early hours of the morning, at five o'clock. She also told me that her mom was in such a state that she wasn't able to travel in the ambulance and my friend travelled instead.

I was amazed when I heard it. It was so strange that I bumped into my friend's sister. I hadn't been in touch or anything and my friend hadn't been in touch either. It wasn't even that my friend had been that close and I wouldn't have been talking to her about her dad that much. She was more of a good acquaintance than a friend.

It also wasn't like I had any reason to see the heart attack coming. My friend's dad hadn't been sick at all. His health had been good up to that. He had no sort of heart complaint or anything. I didn't have any pre-knowledge. It happened out of the blue. I feel it was strange that I dreamt about something that had no real connection to me.

I went home and told my mom. I said, 'What did I tell you this morning? What was my dream about?' She repeated it before I prompted her. She told me the dream as I had told it to her, more or less. I then said, 'You won't believe this but I met one of the family down the town and she told me her father had a heart attack this morning.' My mother couldn't believe it. Even though she is in her late 80s now, I'm sure she remembers it. It was a talking-point among us for years to come.

It was the one strange thing that ever happened to me. Nothing else strange has occurred. I never had any dream like that since and I never had any dream like that about my own family. I wouldn't even be into that sort of thing. I've been to a fortune-teller a couple of times and I think it's the greatest waste of money ever. I think most of it is due to luck. And I wouldn't read my star signs or anything like that.

But this I really feel did happen. I believe, to this day, that I saw it. My only theory is that the brain is amazing and capable of more than we know. There's something there that is beyond our understanding. It's a fascinating thing. Yet this one dream is all that has ever happened to me. But it certainly did happen and, even with the passage of time, I remember it vividly still.

DAVE, A DRIVING INSTRUCTOR FROM DUBLIN, foresaw a car crash that occurred on 1 December 2004.

One night, at the end of November 2004, I dreamt I was in a road traffic accident. The dream had enormous detail. I saw myself tutoring a guy down a country road, checking to see if he could handle the bends and things like that. We were in my Nissan diesel car and it was a bright day. There was foliage on the side of the road.

I think I was wearing a trousers and a shirt and maybe a fawn jumper. There was a person in the dream representing the driver. The person was a male, although it wasn't anyone in particular. I dreamt that we would have an accident on a bend. I also saw a truck. I recall telling the office staff about the dream at the time it happened.

Two days later, on 1 December, I took out a learner driver who was in his mid-30s. He was a confident guy and quite accomplished. It was pleasant weather, at the time, but it had rained earlier and, as a result, the road conditions were a little greasy. I took him in my car, although ironically his next lesson would have been in his own car.

I had planned to take him through the suburbs, but for some reason I decided to give him a lesson involving things like scanning ahead and what's technically called 'tyre grip trade-off'. When you are driving along a straight road you are getting 100 per cent grip with your tyres because they are only performing one function. If, on the other hand, you are caught braking on the apex of a bend, you are splitting your tyre grip 50-50 and you are not in full control.

The lesson is that if you are coming to a bend you do all your braking in the straight so that you are just steering as you enter the bend. In that way you are getting 100 per cent grip. That entailed bringing the guy down back country roads. I chose the back roads from Cappagh Hospital to Blanchardstown in Dublin, which are winding country roads with bends. I was just drawn to take that route.

At 12.30 in the afternoon we were on a longish straight on one of those country roads. There was a sharp, right-hand bend up ahead. At the time I was teaching the guy how to scan ahead and see around the bend before we got to it. I was also teaching him about braking.

At some point I got this image of a car's silhouette about to come around the bend. It suddenly hit me that we were going to crash. I knew what was coming. I knew what was going to happen and that nothing could be done to avoid it. I think I knew, at that moment, that what had been in my dream was going to occur.

It was a Nissan Micra hammering around the corner, with a young guy driving. He hit us at the apex of the bend. The middle of his car hit the area around my right headlamp. We were both totally written off. My bonnet was pushed into the engine. The whole right-hand front of my car was gone. His car was severely damaged too.

It all happened quickly, in milliseconds or microseconds. Everything occurred so fast. I only just had time to get my passenger into a safety position and take over with the dual controls. I also managed to get my car into the ditch on my side of the road. That's why he didn't hit us head-on.

In relation to the other driver's car, he had been skidding for about 100 yards before he reached the bend. He had misjudged what he was doing. The impact of the crash was so severe that his control pedals were bent, so you can imagine the force involved. The momentum was such that his car was pushed back a good 12 feet. My client was mainly OK, although he had some soft tissue damage. I was OK too.

Both cars suddenly started to smoke heavily. I ran over to the other guy and forced open his door. His ankle was caught between the brake and the clutch pedal. I managed, with pure adrenaline, to bend one of the pedals just enough to get his ankle out. A truck then arrived on the scene and I grabbed the guy's tools and opened the bonnets. I used the tools to cut the earth straps and things like that, to help stop the fire. The emergency services eventually arrived.

There had to be a tie-in between the accident and the dream. The parallels were remarkable. The terrain was the same. My car was the same. In both I could see foliage and it was a country road with a turn ahead to the right. The day was bright in both cases. I also saw a truck in the dream. And, of course, there was the crash.

I think that, as a result of the dream, I gained a couple of seconds. That proved invaluable. I was subliminally on guard, there's no question about that. It made me look a little bit earlier and a little bit harder. It meant I was able to act immediately. Don't forget that everything took place in a hair's breadth and I was able to react quickly. I think that, and the skills I had, saved the day.

I believe that my dream was a forewarning. What eventually happened was all in the dream. I couldn't believe it. I didn't go around saying it but it really was a dream that started it all. I think that all three of us were lucky to survive. I got a commendation from the Fire Chief for what I did. I basically saved three lives. At least one of us would have been paraplegic if I hadn't done what I did.

DELIA, FROM COUNTY LOUTH, had a most extraordinary 'flash' preview, or waking image, of her partner's death.

I met Joe in May 2006. I started dating him. It was all very strange. The way we met was very coincidental. Neither of us was supposed to be where we were at the time. Plans had been changed. But, from the moment we met, there was a bond between the two of us. Everything felt very comfortable. I had never experienced it before. It was as if we had known each other for years.

About two weeks after dating him, I got this 'flash' of a scene where I was sitting by his bed in a hospital. I was on the left-hand side of his bed, as you looked at it, and I could see a monitor on the right-hand side. I could see numbers flashing up on it and, because my father was in and out of hospital at the time with a heart complaint, I took it to be a heart monitor.

The whole thing wasn't just visual even though in the 'flash' he was lying there weakened. It was also a 'sense'. I had a sense that he was seriously ill. I felt that there was something wrong with his chest, although there was no reason to feel that from looking at him. I could even feel a sort of heaviness in my own chest, which told me there was something wrong. He was a heavy smoker so, from that time on, I nagged him to go to see a doctor and get something done.

Although there was nothing that seemed to be wrong with him, this particular scene would regularly flash in front of my eyes. It was like the way you would see something in a daydream. I could be sitting and relaxing and I would get a flash of the scene. I could be lying in bed and just about to get up or go to sleep.

We might have been involved in something together, like

shopping, and I would get it. It would stop me in my tracks every time I saw it. I felt very close to him, at the time, and it was like this was coming to me as a warning to say, 'This is ahead of you.'

Time passed by and we had a son. Around the time that our son was born, Joe started taking better care of his health. He had blood tests done and he completely changed his diet. He brought his cholesterol down to a more reasonable level. He was looking well.

He eventually had to go for an X-ray for a sore shoulder. He was complaining of shoulder pain. It was thought that he had just pulled a muscle and all he needed was time for it to heal. It turned out that he had end-stage lung cancer.

Up to that he seemed fine and was able to do a full day's work. We were both completely oblivious to anything being wrong. We were even planning on building a house together. Following the cancer diagnosis, however, he was confined to hospital and he lost a lot of weight. We eventually got married in the hospital. A couple of days later, and just three weeks after he was admitted to hospital, he died. He was 48 years of age.

Just a few days before he died he had been moved into a private room in the hospital. He was on oxygen at that time. I used to sit on the right-hand side of his bed, as you faced it. I was, in other words, on his left. But the morning he died I moved around to the other side of his bed and I sat holding his hands. I moved because it was a small room and it was getting more overcrowded.

From where I sat on the left, I looked over at a monitor on the right-hand side and it was flashing. The premonition had come true! It had been the scene of him dying. The only mistake I had made was thinking in my premonition that it was a heart monitor I was looking over at. It was, in fact, an oxygen monitor. Everything, otherwise, was exactly the same.

I think, looking back, that I was given forewarnings. There is a history of them in my family. My mother is also that way and so were her aunts. It was very acceptable to both my parents that you could have them. It's a thing that we were never frightened of. So I think that's what I had and my fore-warnings were to prepare me for what was ahead, that Joe and I weren't going to grow old together and that his death wouldn't come as such a huge shock to me.

It wasn't the first time that I had them. I had several car accidents over the years and I would also have had flashes ahead of them. Those flashes were of the couple of seconds before the car I was in crashed. They might be of me hitting a silver car and eventually I would have an accident where I would hit that exact sort of car. I would have them for maybe a month beforehand. They would be very short, very clear and very vivid, like a YouTube clip.

In those crash scenes I was directly involved, driving the car. But in the scene where Joe died I was standing back watching. I wasn't really in it, even though I knew it was me sitting by his bedside. I was looking after him.

I feel that was my whole role in Joe's life – to take care of him and to ensure that he had the best he could get. That's the bigger picture I think I was part of. Life is not just a series of random events. There are certain people we are meant to cross paths with and I think our paths were destined to cross.

SHEELAGH, FROM COUNTY ANTRIM, was forewarned of an unexpected gynaecological operation and the surgeon who would perform it. The year was 1978.

I went to bed, one night, feeling fine. I fell asleep as normal. During the night I had a dream. It was multicoloured and very realistic. I honestly don't know what time of night it was. I dreamt that I was being admitted to hospital, for an operation, and that when I went into the theatre this particular surgeon, who I never saw before, was there. He was waiting in his green cap and green gown, ready to operate on me.

I could see myself being transported from the ante-room, where I had been prepared, into the theatre. I was wearing a gown, lying on this trolley. I was looking up and saw the surgeon. Although I had never seen him before, his features were very vivid. He was completely scrubbed up, ready for the operation. He was standing there, smoking a cigarette. All I could think was, 'The cheek of him, standing there and smoking!' Somehow I knew that it was all related to something gynaecological.

When I was in the bathroom the next morning I thought, 'That was peculiar what I dreamt about last night.' I also discovered I was having a bleed. I then put it out of my head and went off to the office, to work. During the morning I didn't feel too well. I felt fatigued. I thought I might have been tired because of my dream and because I didn't sleep well. I even started thinking it might have been stress but it wasn't.

I told one of my colleagues, 'I don't feel too good, maybe I should go home.' She said, 'Maybe it's the flu.' I said it wasn't. She asked me about my symptoms and I explained to her how I felt. She then asked me who my GP was and she rang him up. He said, 'Tell her to come up right away.' I think he was anxious, thinking that because of the bleed it might have been something cancer-related.

I got into the car and went right away to my GP's surgery. He was waiting there for me. He examined me and said, 'You need to have an emergency meeting with a gynaecologist.' He arranged for me to have a private visit with a consultant that I had never met before. It wasn't the same gynaecologist I had when my son was born. The appointment was arranged for the very next morning at the hospital, where he had his private rooms.

The gynaecologist eventually arrived. He came out to the waiting-room and he called me. I just looked at him. It was astounding. It was the exact same person I saw in my dream. I knew immediately, 'That's the man I saw!' There he was. I couldn't believe it. I was taken aback.

He wasn't wearing scrubs, like I saw in my dream. Instead he was in a lounge suit. He had the same black, wavy hair. He wasn't tall, only about 5ft 4in. I got a shock. My mind started racing and I thought, 'What's next?'

He examined me and said, 'I will have to bring you in and have a better look, to see what's going on. If I see anything wrong during the operation, I may have to do a hysterectomy.' I agreed and I replied, 'That's fine.' I was in the hospital, for the operation, within a week. I remember going in on a Monday and was due into the theatre on the Tuesday, the following day.

On the Tuesday, as I was being wheeled into the theatre from the ante-room, all the rest of my dream came true. The same consultant was standing there but he was now in his scrubs. He was between the ante-room and the theatre, wearing a green cap and gown, identical to what I saw in my dream. He was even smoking, again exactly as in my dream. It was all precisely the same as I had dreamt.

It was all so very peculiar, a very strange thing, really astounding. Everything that happened came true. People come up with all sorts of reasons – that it's your subconscious or something prehistoric. But, whatever it was, I did see exactly what was ahead involving this man that I didn't know and had never met. Somehow he appeared in my dream because eventually, in reality, that's what was going to happen – that I was going to see him.

I really don't know where it comes from. My maternal grandmother was very susceptible to getting feelings about things and could foretell things. I didn't know her well because I was only 14 when she died and she had lived a good bit away from us. But, as a result, I often wonder did I inherit it? Was there something in the family?

My aunt also had this ability. She told me once that my uncle was away in England and she had an awful dream about him not being very well. She said that she went to bed, one afternoon, and her mother came to her. Her mother had been dead a long time, at that stage. She came to her and told her, 'Don't worry! Everything will be alright!' When my uncle came home, it turned out that he wasn't very well. He had to go into hospital but he was OK.

So maybe there's a family connection. Sometimes I wonder. I still think back on what happened, not very often but there are times when I think, 'How very strange!' Thankfully, at least, all was well afterwards from the medical side. There was just a tiny problem that had to be fixed. I eventually went back to the consultant and he gave me the all-clear. I got to know him quite well but I never told him about my dream. He might have thought, 'I have a right one here!'

MARIE, FROM NEW YORK, studied in Dublin in the early 1970s, where she had a strange predictive dream. It is one of the many dreams and forewarnings she has experienced in her life.

I decided to go to Ireland, to study at UCD, after I finished law school in the States. I hadn't been in a Catholic church for about ten years. I was the rebel in my family and had stopped going to church because I didn't believe in it. I did, however, find the idea of the Cistercians or the Trappists – the contemplative life – to be very interesting.

112

During one Easter vacation in Dublin I said, 'Let me try something connected to the contemplative life.' My father's people had been from Moycullen, in County Galway, but had left during the Famine. There was a monastery nearby and I called them up and asked, 'Can I come for the weekend?' The head of the monastery said, 'Sure, come along. We have 21 farmers' wives, from County Clare, doing a retreat but you're welcome to join us.'

A lovely priest picked me up at the nearby railway station. His greeting was very warm. I was telling him that I had been in the Peace Corps and had travelled a lot, and he started saying how he had always wanted to be a missionary in Brazil. He was a lovely man. At the monastery there was another priest who told me that he had spent the previous summer helping out in a parish in Kingston, New York, where my father was born.

There was also a nun there, whose first language was French. I told her about some wonderful nuns I had met in the South of France. There were all sorts of signs that made me feel I was supposed to be there, and there were lots of things happening that were telling me, 'This is a good place to be.'

I had a wonderful time at the monastery. I listened to all the farmers' wives and all they had to say, which was fascinating. I went to confession for the first time in ten years and took communion. I even stayed on a couple of days after the farmers' wives left. I felt so totally at home. I eventually took the train back to Dublin.

That night – my first night back – I had a dream. There was a 40-foot tidal wave and I was beneath it. I looked up at it and I said, 'God! I'm sorry! This one's too big and I don't have the strength to fight anymore!' So I just gave up. The next thing, in my dream, I was coming up on the shore, out of the water, and I realised, 'Oh, my God! I've survived this! I'm going to live!' I was in total shock that I had lived.

After I emerged on the shore I looked up at a hill ahead of me and I saw this house. It was a lovely little house, with red shutters. The roof was of a very traditional style typical of old Quebec. It was a small, quaint house and was very beautiful, sitting there by itself. It was very distinctive and looked like a place I should get to. That was the end of the dream.

I eventually finished at UCD and moved back home. The after-effects of my visit to the monastery stayed with me. I started going to mass again and I've been doing it ever since. The retreat in Ireland made me believe that I didn't have to have the same kind of faith my parents had. The head of the monastery had been fabulous, as had the nun. The retreat had been a revelation.

I moved, in time, to Montreal and lived in the middle of the city, on the nineteenth floor. Then, in June 1981, a friend came up to me and said, 'Have I found the house for you!' She said, 'This is the house you should live in. You'll love it.' It was way out in the country, in the middle of nowhere. I went out to see it. When you came up to it from the back it looked like just any house. But when I saw it from the front it was exactly the same house I had seen in my dream!

The house was up on the top of a hill, with red shutters. It was the same type of roof I had seen in the dream. The house was sitting there by itself. It was built from the wood of old log cabins and the logs were grey-coloured because they were aged. It was very small and extremely beautiful. It had a huge valley and big forest in front of it. It was the identical house.

From the moment I looked at it I realised, 'That was the house I saw on the hill in my dream.' I immediately made the connection. The only difference was that whereas in my dream the house looked out on the ocean, here it looked out on a big valley and a huge forest. I felt, 'I'm supposed to be here.' I took the house and lived there for a full year.

I then thought to myself, 'What has happened must mean something.' But I didn't know what it meant. I think the reason I dreamt of the tidal wave was because I had spent many years going against the flow. I was always standing up for myself, most probably with an intense sense of self-righteousness. I was always fighting someone on issues of justice. I think my surviving the tidal wave represented my coming back into the fold. It was a survival dream. And the house was where I was eventually meant to be.

I had another dream relating to a tidal wave at a much later stage. This one concerned the tsunami in Thailand, in December 2004. My husband's son lives in Bangkok, with his Thai wife, and has done so for decades. We were visiting them at the time. We ended up staying in a hotel outside a place called Krabi.

One night I had a dream that I fell into a klong, which is one of the canals in Bangkok. I don't know how I fell in but I went down to the bottom. I said, 'I'm not going to die here!' So I slammed down on my feet and I pushed up as hard as I could. That dream happened the night before the tsunami.

The tsunami hit Thailand on 26 December 2004. It was a beautiful, sunny day. The water started rising and it was moving up to our hotel. All around us there was a lot of destruction. The fishermen lost their boats. Some hotels were destroyed. The manager of our hotel, who was away at the time of the tsunami, phoned and said, 'Evacuate everybody!' Our hotel was right in front of a national park, which was on a big hill, and that's where we went.

It was all very odd. It's not so much that I saw what was coming because falling into the klong wasn't exactly the same as facing a tsunami. But it all concerned drowning in water and I did say, 'I'm not going to die here!' I believe that was connected to what was going to happen the next day.

I have had many premonitions throughout my life. I've had many things happen where I knew what was happening before it occurred. I've known I was in danger. I've known people were coming. I've known lots of things like that, that I shouldn't have known but I profoundly knew.

I was, for instance, very close to my grandfather. Back in the 1960s I lived in Africa, where I taught. There wasn't any email at the time and communication was impossible. I didn't speak to my family for two years. Yet, one night, I felt, 'I know something is wrong with my grandfather.' I wrote down the date in my diary. It turned out that he had a stroke that night.

Many years later, when I was in law school, I woke up during the night and again I thought, 'Something is wrong with my grandfather.' I knew I shouldn't go to school, so I went to the train station instead. Again, sure enough, he had a stroke. I had known on both occasions that something was wrong.

When my grandfather did die, on the other hand, my father called me. It was before the spring break. My father said, 'Your grandfather is not well. Maybe you should come.' I said, 'Don't worry. I'm very close to him. If anything is really wrong, I will know and I will come. Otherwise I will wait until the spring break and I will go down and see him then.' He died that night. So, that time, I didn't know, whereas on the two earlier occasions, ten years apart, I did know.

I don't know what these things are. I don't understand them and I have no explanations. I just know they are there. There have been times when I've felt very connected. But it happens much less now. At this stage of my life I don't feel the same level of awareness that I have sometimes felt. Who knows why that should be so?

I suspect some people are more skilled at this sort of thing than others. I also suspect that we all have more skills than we are aware of but don't know how to use them. I have all sorts of beliefs like that. But I have to say that I don't really know what causes these things. I just can't explain them.

 EILEEN, FROM COUNTY LOUTH, **has had many dreams including one about her father, which occurred just days after Christmas 1993.**

I remember the dream about my dad. He was at the bottom of a hill, where my uncle lives in Donegal. It was like at the bottom of a hilly drive, with a bit of a bend in it. There are bushes on one side and shrubs on the other. It's in the country and there's a good incline on the hill. My dad was struggling to walk up.

I was at the front window of my uncle's house, looking down at my dad. I was standing at this big front window and my dad was looking at me as if to say, 'I can't get up!' The expression in his face was telling me he was struggling. I was wondering why. I thought, 'That would never be him.' I knew that dream meant something but I couldn't figure it out at the time. I did, however, wonder about it afterwards.

A few days later my dad and my mum came to visit me. Christmas week had just passed. I remember seeing their car coming down the street and I was wondering, 'Why are they here on a Tuesday?' It was most unusual. Something was already telling me that all wasn't well. I got the feeling, 'Something is wrong!'

We went into the house and nobody said anything for a few minutes. My mum then started talking and she said, 'Your dad went to the doctor and they want to send him for

X-rays.' This was the first time he had been to the doctor or a dentist. He had all his teeth, had only smoked when he was young, was a good-living man and didn't drink. My parents then said that it could be TB or bronchitis or a tumour or whatever.

It turned out to be the worst of those options – a tumour in the lung. The minute I heard it, I connected the dream with my dad. I said, 'That was the meaning of that dream!' I immediately knew that the dream was about my dad struggling. It was telling me that he had a struggle ahead of him. And he did. He died 11 months later.

I have had many other dreams in my life. We lived, for a time, in Glasgow. I dreamt that the woman who lived across the road from us had broken her arm. She lived up in a top flat. I dreamt I was looking over at her veranda and I could see her with a big cast on her arm. I told my mum and she laughed at me.

That night I came home from school and my mum said, 'Wait till you hear!' She told me that the woman across from us had a broken arm. She had only broken it that day. I forget exactly what had happened but she had broken it. My mother was astonished. I think she said, 'There's something like the black cat about you.' She was laughing.

Another time, when I was working, I had a dream that there was a coloured man in my workplace. I was terrified. There weren't that many coloured people about at the time and it frightened me. It's not like today. I told my mum and I said to her, 'But there are no coloured people at work.'

I went into work that day – I think it was a Monday – and I had to use a photocopier. I had to photocopy the sheets with the work for the mechanics and people like that to do that week. I went over to the building where I usually did the photocopying but the machine was broken. Instead I went over to another building.

I was standing there in a big, lonely room, with two big whoppers of machines in it. The door suddenly opened and in came this big coloured man. I was absolutely terrified. I wasn't used to it. I had loads to photocopy so it wasn't like I could leave in a minute.

I remember going home and telling my mum and we were laughing about the way it had come about. If the machine hadn't been broken in the other place, I would never have seen him. He was a salesman, apparently, and someone had sent him in to get something done. I suppose there was no big deal about what happened but I had seen it coming.

I had another dream, about my brother. I had it at least three times. I saw that he was in the garden and his wife had put him there to live. It seemed bizarre. The garden was split down the middle. By the time I had the dream twice I thought, 'There's something to this dream.' I wondered why I was getting it.

One night, weeks later, I was coming home from my mum's and my sister remarked to me, 'Isn't that terrible about our brother?' I said, 'What do you mean?' She told me that the marriage was over and they were splitting everything down the middle. I said, 'What?' It was such a shock. They eventually got divorced. I knew it was coming.

I always remember my dreams. I remember them precisely. I have no doubt they are telling me something. I have too many of them to dismiss them. I believe they come from your people who go before you. They are the ones telling you what you see. There's only a veil – a net curtain – between us. I think they are with us and they warn us of what is to come.

ANTHONY, FROM COUNTY CORK, **had a recurring dream that invariably came true.**

Starting in the late 1960s, I had a recurring dream which was so intense that it would often wake me up. It went on for ages and ages, from the late 1960s into the 1970s. It got to a stage where I'd wake and say, 'Here we go again!' The dream was always the same. I lived in the country and our house faced south. It would be a sunny day. An aircraft would come into view and it would crash and explode.

It wasn't always the same type of plane, although it was usually a small twin-engine aircraft. It was never a huge plane. But it would crash within the horizon of a field down below our house. It was always on the south side of the house.

I would, in a lot of cases, rush to the scene of the crash. There would often be casualties, although I never got involved with them. Instead I'd be ringing the fire services and things like that. This happened to me over and over again.

It's not really that the dream was horrifying – it's just that it was remarkably realistic and it involved something that was happening. It's like being at the scene of a road accident – you don't have time to be horrified, you just get involved. You are reacting because you are the only person there. You are active and doing things.

The strange thing was that when I'd wake up in the morning and I'd turn on the news or read the papers, there would be reports of an air crash. This would always happen. Over a couple of days following the dream, invariably there would also be three major air crashes somewhere around the world. I started to feel guilty about this and asked myself, 'I wonder is there somebody I can contact, to warn them?'

One night I had the dream and again the aircraft exploded

in front of me. I literally jumped up in the bed and I thought I had been burned. I looked at my arm. On my right arm there were three little spots, as if somebody put a burning surface or sprinkled liquid on it. It felt like someone had sprinkled hot water or hot oil on my arm. I asked my wife, 'Did you spill something on me?' But she hadn't. It was strange. I still have the spots to this day.

I moved eventually to Dublin but my father still lived at home. One day I came home on a visit. We were making hay, out in the field, and I was sitting with my father. We were having a cup of tea. An aircraft passed overhead. He suddenly said to me, 'Did I ever tell you of a dream I used to have?' He had my attention immediately. I said, 'No, what was the dream?'

My father said, 'I often had a dream of an aircraft crashing below the house, down in the field.' It was exactly the same location as in my dream. He said, 'It's always the same dream. The aircraft crashes. I'm out catching the horse and I have a rope in my hand. But the flames from the plane are so hot that I can't go near it. I often throw the horse's reins into the aircraft, to rescue people from the flames.'

I was absolutely dumbfounded. My father wasn't the type of person to exaggerate or make things up. He was a very practical person and wasn't given to flights of fancy. He had his feet on the ground. Yet here he was having the same dream that I was after having myself. I told him, 'You're not going to believe this but I've had the same dream.'

I eventually had a son. One morning my wife and I were sitting down and having breakfast. It might have been during summertime, during the holidays. The little fellow came down at about 9.30 or so. I remember it was a beautiful day. I said, 'How are you? How are things today?' He said, 'I had a very funny dream.' I said, 'What was it about?'

He said, 'I was at home with Granddad and an airplane came along, over the house, and came down into the field where it crashed and went up in flames.' My wife knew of my dream, because I had told her, so we looked at each other and rolled our eyes to heaven. When he left the room we wondered, 'God almighty! What's going on?'

This was the third generation having that very same dream. My father hadn't realised that my son had it. My son didn't realise that my father had it. None of us realised that the other had the dream. I never asked my son about it again but for his sake I hope it never recurred. I also never spoke to my father about it again.

What I find strange, though, is that there's a connection between our dreams and the number three. When I had the dream it would be followed by three crashes. There were also three generations – my father, myself and my son. There were, additionally, the three burns on my arm. Three seems to have something to do with it. There was some sort of connection. Don't ask me why.

I still have dreams, the same as anybody else. I have good dreams and bad dreams, probably the normal pattern that you'd find with everybody. I wouldn't claim to be anything different. I don't jump up after every night claiming to have had different dreams. But I don't have the recurring dream anymore.

I'm relieved I don't have it because I used to feel so guilty when it occurred. I wondered, 'If I knew something was going to happen, why couldn't I do something about it?' After each one I also felt that I had to sit back, for the next couple of days, and watch the papers to see about air crashes. I'm glad that's gone, at least.

DIANA, WHO LIVES IN COUNTY TIPPERARY, has had the ability, since childhood, to see images or pictures of future events.

Ever since I was a small child pictures would come to me that would eventually be realised. What would happen, for no good reason whatsoever, was that a picture would suddenly appear in my mind. I'd get it anytime, completely out of the blue and unexpectedly. It would emerge out of nothing and I would have no idea how it would be realised, how it would click into place.·

I think my first experience goes back to when I was very young, very small. I was born in London, during the Blitz, and didn't come to Ireland until I was about five years old. My earliest memories are of war. I think I had them at that stage. People used to say, 'We always know it's going to be a bad air raid because Diana can't sleep.' If I wasn't settled they would look out. I obviously had them even then.

The pictures could be about almost anything. They were just 'pictures'. No words were involved. I could be doing absolutely anything and a picture would come into my mind. It might not make sense to me, initially, but I would store it. Sometimes it would be realised sooner; other times it would take longer. But they would all happen sooner or later. Then, when it would be realised, I would think, 'Ah! That's what it was all about!'

There was no sense of foreboding with any of the ones I ever had. I had a friend who had a most horrendous dream or vision of the Zeebrugge ferry disaster. She had it around the time that the disaster was taking place. That was obviously something that really frightened her. But mine were never of that nature. I also never worried about them when they came.

It was just that I might see something odd and then it would be realised.

I experienced one of the strangest in the mid-1970s. This one was a picture of a red carpet with gold-like scrolls on it. The pattern on the carpet was very distinct. It was a good-quality carpet and I had never seen the pattern before. It was very different. I was extremely surprised when the picture came and I hadn't the slightest idea what it was about. The last thing I expected was to see a picture of a carpet. I do remember it because it was so unusual and dramatic and it stood out so clearly.

I would sometimes share the experience with other people and, because what I saw was so odd, I think I did so in this case. Although I can't remember exactly when or where the picture of the carpet cropped up, I think I mentioned it to some people. I had friends that I could say something like that to. I felt I could share it with them. I think they took the view that I did – wait and see what happens!

About two years later I ended up in court, with custody issues, after my marriage broke down. I was back in the UK at this stage. It was evening time, about five o'clock. I was walking with my barrister and my solicitor and for some reason we went into his chambers, which had a pretty heavy door. The door opened and we went up a few stairs. I suddenly saw the exact same carpet. It was identical – red with the unusual gold-like scrolls.

I was a bit shocked to begin with. As I walked along the corridor I could see it more clearly. It wasn't right across the floor; it was going down the middle like a stairs carpet. It seemed like it was good quality, although I didn't spot the make of it. It may have been individually designed. But I was absolutely sure that this was the same carpet. I had never seen one like it before and I have never seen one since.

What happened certainly wasn't a coincidence. I can't believe that. The picture was too unusual and the carpet was unique. I had never seen as odd a carpet before. None of the other pictures I had were as strange as this. For it to be absolutely the same carpet puts it beyond coincidence. I would spot if it was coincidence and it definitely wasn't so.

That was probably the most dramatic one that has ever happened to me. I remember it very distinctly. Many of the others would fit in exactly but this one fitted in unexpectedly, in the oddest of ways. It turned out that the judge had been a barrister in those chambers. Whether that had anything to do with it or not, I don't know. It was very strange, either way.

They don't happen anymore. I haven't had one in a long time. The last one I had was about ten or eleven years ago. A friend of mine wanted to get pregnant. She had been hoping for many years and was almost beyond hope. I had a picture of a little girl of about nine years of age, with plaits, who was the image of her mother. I told her and I told other friends also.

My friend then got pregnant and had a baby girl. The baby bore far more resemblance to her father than to her mother for years. But she is now nine years of age, often has plaits, and is the image of her mother. I think that is the last picture I've had.

I have no idea what these things are. Because I have a strong Christian faith, I always thought of them as being Christian prophecy. They were some sort of reassurance to me that I was on the right track. I never tried to explain them. I suppose I just ran with them and accepted them. I also never tried to cultivate them. Once the picture was realised it receded. That's what always happened. And something else would crop up.

ANGELA, WHO LIVES IN LIMERICK, had a worrying dream about her twin sister's pregnancy. It happened in the mid-2000s.

My twin sister was in her late 30s at the time. She was about two or three months into her pregnancy. It was her second child and she hadn't had any problems with the first one. All had gone perfectly well with that. There was nothing to indicate that anything might go wrong with the second birth either.

I had this dream, one night, when I was asleep. In the dream I could see my sister lying on a sofa and it was very hard for her to move around. She was struggling and quite ill. She looked tired and worn out. The dream was very real and lifelike. I got the feeling from it that she needed to take it easy or she could lose the baby.

I woke up, the next morning, and was worried. I felt I had better ring her. I didn't want to freak her out but I thought I had better let her know. I said to her, 'You will probably think I'm crazy but I just had a dream about you and I am worried.' I went into the basics of the dream and told her that I saw her lying on a sofa and she wasn't well. I warned her to take it easy and said, 'It will be a difficult pregnancy. Rest up.'

It was only then that she confirmed that she had been told by her doctor to take it easy. I hadn't known that at the time. She was feeling tired but she didn't think there was anything serious wrong. Later on, sometime after we talked, she was told she had developed diabetes. It can happen in pregnancy and it could have been dangerous.

I had no idea, when we spoke, that it was becoming a difficult pregnancy for her. Neither of us, at that stage, knew of the diabetes. It eventually made her tired and a bit sluggish, like she was in my dream. She also had to inject herself and got a bit fed up having to do that. Even though the diabetes disappeared after she had the baby, she was told that she couldn't have any more children.

My sister took what I said on board and appreciated my saying it. I think it helped her a bit. She took it easier and eventually the baby – a little girl – was born. It was a difficult birth but all was OK, everything was just fine. Afterwards, however, the child did have problems with its hip and had to go in and out of hospital a lot to get it sorted out.

That was the end of what happened and we never spoke about it again. I don't think it had anything to do with us being twins. I don't really get that sort of thing. I know other twins say that they know it when their twin is in pain or something is wrong. I sometimes get something a bit like that but I don't get it to the same level that other twins report it.

Instead, in the case of the pregnancy, I think that what I saw in my dream was different. I think it was a genuine forewarning. I think, somehow, that I was meant to see what was happening to my sister and to get her to slow down a bit. And it helped.

I have had other forewarnings as well. One time I had a dream about a hotel. I saw wallpaper, which was a creamy-beige colour and had little flecks of gold going through it, with swirls and things like that. I also saw the room, which had a grey-beige carpet but was nothing exceptional. It was the wallpaper that stood out. It was very distinctive.

I thought nothing of it at the time. I felt it was just an ordinary dream. But I was in Poland on a holiday, about two years later, and I was in the exact same room. Everything was identical. It was the exact same hotel and the exact same wallpaper. When I saw it I knew I had seen it before. I realised where I had seen it – in my dream! I was blown away by that.

I've had more too. I had one about a country road and

later found myself on the exact same road. I have had ones about being robbed or about a row. I have had one about the funeral of a member of my family and I saw who was at it. I didn't like that very much. It often takes years before they become reality.

Whenever I have a forewarning, it comes as a dream. I can usually tell the difference between it and an ordinary dream. It took me a while to figure it out. But I did so over the years and I know the difference now. It's just a very distinct feeling I get inside. It's hard to explain but I know they are real.

Sometimes, however, I am not aware of the dreams being forewarnings at the time I have them. The ones in the hotel in Poland or going down the country lane, for example, I wasn't aware of them being forewarnings at the time I dreamt them. Mostly, however, I know what they are. And then they almost always happen.

Sometimes they come in the opposite way. I might, for example, get a forewarning that I am going to meet my sister but it would be a friend I would unexpectedly meet. I would meet them soon after. And, when I meet them, I know it was they who were indicated to me in my dream. It's hard to explain. It's just a 'knowing' feeling.

I think it's a gift I have. I believe I get them to help myself or to help other people. I don't consider myself psychic or anything like that. It's just that sometimes I get them. And when I have them, I trust in them. I won't do things if I have a bad warning about them. The forewarning is enough for me.

MARY, FROM COUNTY ANTRIM, had intimations that her brother was battling a life-threatening illness. It happened in the early 1960s.

I was on holiday in Donegal, staying in my aunt's house for three weeks. I was with my sister and one of my brothers.

While I was there I had the weirdest dream about an older brother of mine. I had eight brothers but he was the one above me. At the time of my dream I was about 16 years of age and he was around 20. He was working over in Wales.

In my dream I could see inside a church. It was the church down in Drogheda, with St. Oliver Plunkett's relics. My mum always took my brother there, every year, because he had TB as a child. When he was three years of age, as a result of the TB they had to take his kneecap away. I had never seen the church because she could only afford to take him down. But I knew that's where he was.

In my dream I was kneeling alongside my brother in the church. My mum was in front of him. My brother was trying to kneel down and he was crying. I was looking at this. That was something he couldn't do in reality because he had no kneecap. The doctors had been able to release tendons at the back of the knee, to give him mobility and to make him not so short in the leg, but he couldn't bend his knee.

He eventually knelt down, although he was screaming with pain. He was in agony. I was grabbing at my mother and trying to get her attention. I was trying to tell her, 'Look, he's crying and he's kneeling! Turn around! Turn around! Take a look! Take a look! He's kneeling!' But my mum was ignoring me. It was strange.

When I woke up I knew there was something wrong. I was very worried. I told my sister about the dream but she dismissed it. She didn't want to know. There were no phones nearby where I could call my mother. I also couldn't hop on a bus and come home. I just didn't settle in the days afterwards.

I had to wait about seven days before I got on the bus and came home. When I came in my mum wasn't there. My older brothers were there instead. I asked them, 'Where's Mum?' They said, 'She took the younger ones on holiday down to

County Louth.' I thought, 'God! I can't even tell her.' I asked them, 'There isn't, by any chance, a letter for me from our brother in Wales?' They said there wasn't. But one of them then said, 'There is a telegram over there.'

I went over to the clock and grabbed the telegram. I ran down to my chum's house and we opened it. The message said that my brother was in hospital and had developed peritonitis as a result of appendicitis. The telegram was sent to say that he mightn't live. We didn't have a phone in our home then, but we found one and we called the hospital. They gave us a number for the recovery home where he had been sent to. I got talking to him and eventually he got his health back again.

To me that dream was very significant. There was nothing on my mind to do with my brother when I was in Donegal. My brother was not in my head. I was too busy going to dances and enjoying myself with a whole load of fellows who were from Belfast and who were friends of the family. So my brother was the furthest thing from my mind. He was way down the list.

Maybe it was because we were close. I was next down to my brother. When he went into hospital with TB as a child, my mother was pregnant with my sister. He knew I was there for him but my mother wasn't there. Later, if I had wanted to go to a dance he took me along with his friends. I think there was some connection.

I believe what happened was some sort of warning. It was something that came to me. If you want to call it telepathy you can. He was definitely sick at the same time as I had the dream. He was dying and they weren't sure they were going to be able to get him back.

Even when I had come home from Donegal, my mum wasn't there. It explained for me how, when I was trying to contact her in the dream, she was kind of dismissive and couldn't be got. It was also years later before I set foot in the church in Drogheda.

My brother eventually ended up living in Canada, where he died at the age of 66. Leading up to the Christmas when he died, every time I came into my house I would smell smoke. It wasn't the smoke of burning but the smoke of cigarettes. I'd be sitting by the fireplace and I'd ask my friend, 'Can you smell cigarette smoke?' She'd say, 'No. You're imagining things.' But it went on for a couple of weeks. There was a sort of oddness about the whole thing.

Christmas came and passed by. The New Year came and went. My uncle eventually came up from Donegal, staying with my younger brother. One day my younger brother phoned me. I thought he was about to tell me that we were going to have a bit of a shindig because my uncle was up. But he told me, 'I'm sorry. I didn't know whether to come up to you or to ask you to come down to me, to tell you.' I said, 'Tell me what?'

He told me that my brother had been found dead in Canada. He had died just before Christmas. I then realised what the cigarette smoke was all about. He was a shocking cigarette smoker. It was at the same time that he had died that I had smelled the cigarette smoke.

Yet it's the dream that I remember the most. I think it was warning me that my brother was dying and that, at that stage, he needed help. He needed us to know that he was in danger. I have no doubt that there was a connection between that and the dream.

I believe he was trying to contact me – or someone was contacting me – to let me know that my brother was in danger and needed help. I definitely think it was some sort of forewarning of what was happening at the time.

BEVERLEY, WHO COMES FROM CANADA but who now lives in County Down, has dreamt of many extraordinary future events.

The first dream that I can remember happened in late 1983. I was aged 20, at the time, and was living in Canada. The thing about my dreams was that they were always disturbing and detailed. That was especially true about this first one, which involved an air crash. I have always loved planes. I suppose I am fascinated by jet travel and was a flight attendant for a while, later on.

My dream was about an airplane crash which happened somewhere in Europe. I understood that the airline, from its colours, was Alitalia. Because of that I thought the location might have been Italy. The plane had crashed in a forest and there were bodies hanging from the trees. The police had put yellow tape around the forest because people were coming along and trying to have sexual relations with the dead bodies. It was horrific.

It was a very vivid dream. There were lots of bodies, limbs and heads that I could see. Yet it didn't matter to the people coming in what was left of the bodies or what they did to them. In my dream the police were desperately trying to keep these people away. It was like a horrible nightmare. I never had a dream like that before. I wondered, 'How could this happen? Could people really sink that low?'

I woke up and told my mom about it and she told another relative. Then, about two or three weeks later, I saw in the papers that there had been a crash in a forest near Sofia in Bulgaria. The plane belonged to Balkan Bulgarian Airlines. There were bodies hanging from the trees and the police had put tape around the forest because people were coming to loot the bodies. I think I read about it in the *Toronto Star*.

The key points were the same – the crash in Europe, the forest, the bodies hanging from the trees, the police with the tape and the people trying to get at the bodies. Instead of sexual relations, however, it was looting. But the colours of Alitalia and the Bulgarian airline were the same – green and red. I had only thought it was Alitalia because of the colours and again I thought it might have been in Italy for the same reason. All the other main details were the same.

It gave me confirmation that what I had seen in my dream was true. The seed was there, although the precise details differed. I knew, once I saw it in the papers, that there was something to it and that what I had seen in my dream was what eventually happened.

My mom also remarked on it because almost everything I described was so accurate. I probably felt, at the time, that I might have been blowing it out of proportion, but as the years went on and I've had other dreams I realised that what happened was significant and wasn't a one-off.

The next one I remember happened when I was into my 20s. It involved the SkyDome in Toronto, which was a new stadium that was being built at the time. In the dream there were three men who were telephone workers. They somehow had got separated from the ladders or whatever they were on. They were clinging for dear life onto the telephone lines. They were hanging on and hanging on. Two of them eventually fell. The last one was still hanging on but then he dropped too.

It wasn't that long, maybe a week later, that there was an industrial accident at the SkyDome. Two construction workers fell from heights and were killed instantly. I recall that there was a third worker as well and he ended up in hospital. What happened was almost exactly the same as in my dream. I thought, 'Gee! That's what that was about!' I had once again told my mom about that dream beforehand and, after the accident, she said, 'You've definitely got something going on there.'

Another one of my dreams I call 'the man and the cheese' dream. I was aged about 24 or 25 at this stage. My mom is divorced and I always hoped she would find somebody else. We all lived in a big house, at the time, and there were lots of people coming and going. In this dream a suitor came to the door for my mother.

I opened the door and he asked me if my mother was there. I said, 'No, she isn't.' He said, 'That's a shame because I've brought a gift for her.' I was thinking it was going to be something extravagant but he handed me a gift box of cheese, with different cheeses and crackers in it. He then said, 'I'd really like if you would put that away for her in the fridge.' That was the end of the dream.

About a month later my brother came to the door. He was a student at the time. I think it was around my mother's birthday. He said, 'Is Mom there?' She was asleep. I said, 'No, she's sleeping.' He said, 'Can I leave this here for her?' It was a box of cheese. It was exactly the same type of variety box, with a few types of hard and soft cheeses and some crackers. So, just like in my dream, a man called with a box of cheese, although it wasn't a suitor, it was just my brother.

A number of things were interesting though. It was, for a start, most unusual for anyone to call to the door with a box of cheese. It was also not just that it was a box of cheese but that my mother wasn't available. Somebody had also called for her and asked if I would put it away for her. It didn't come right away to me but it dawned on me a couple of hours later, 'Here it goes again!'

My last dream I call 'the man with half a head' dream. This one happened very recently, here in Ireland. I am still single and this was a strange, wistful dream. In the dream I met this guy and we hit it off. I thought he was everything looks-wise and humour-wise and intelligence-wise, only that he always wore this woollen hat. It was a cheap, plain, simple, navy woollen hat.

Just at the moment when we had decided that everything was on and we were going to have a relationship, he lifted off this hat and I saw that he had half a head. From just over his eyebrows it went straight back for about four inches and then it gradually lifted up and it peaked. There was a small point at the crown. So, while he was the perfect man, he had only half a head.

I told my sister about it the next day. I said, 'Would you believe that I met the man of my dreams but there was a catch – he only had half a head!' Then, about a month later, I opened a newspaper and turned one of the pages and the very man of my dreams was there. He was a criminal in England. He was pictured and you could see he had half a head and the police called him 'Mr. Half a Head.' It was him down to the smallest molecule.

That, to me, was the strongest confirmation that what I had seen in my dream was real. I had never seen this guy before in my life. I didn't even know anyone could live looking like this. You wouldn't even know that a brain could be in there. He had seemingly lost part of his head in an accident. But it was exactly what I had seen in my dream. So the joke now is that I have to track him down and see if we are made for each other!

I really don't know what to think of these dreams. It's hard to say. They don't really affect me in everyday life other than that I think, 'Boy! This is something that is there in me and something might come up again!' I wonder whether the dreams have something to do with parallel time-bands or parallel universes, whether you cross over into one. I've sometimes used that to explain my happenings. But I really don't know.

I'm not afraid of the dreams but I don't welcome them either. The only time they might worry me is if they were about people close to me. I wouldn't like that. I wouldn't like to be worried about telling people what I had seen or I wouldn't like it if I became afraid to leave the house. I've been lucky with the ones I have had, so I wouldn't call them a curse. I think instead that they are a little window on a world that you don't normally see.

JOHN, FROM COUNTY LIMERICK, had a dream about death. Within six weeks the precise details of his dream had come to pass. The event happened in 2006.

I had a dream about six weeks before my mother died. It happened on an ordinary night. I hadn't been drinking coffee or anything like that. The dream was in black and white. It was weird. I was looking down from the sky. It was like astral travel, as if I was floating outside of my body. There was a group of people around a grave. The group was about the size that you'd expect at a funeral, 60 or 70 people.

It was a really nice, bright day. I could see a coffin being lowered down. I was standing exactly at the foot of the grave. I could see somebody – a blonde girl – coming over and putting her arms around me and saying, 'You'll be alright, John.' She was dressed in black. She came over to me as the coffin was being lowered. Her blonde hair really stood out in the black-and-white dream.

The next day the dream stuck in my mind. I was surprised. I wondered, 'What could that be about?' All day I thought about it. I never thought of my mother, although she had been sick for a while. Her health hadn't deteriorated, at that stage, and I had no reason to think it was her. The dream then faded away over the weeks.

Six weeks afterwards my mother died and I found myself standing at the very same grave. It was exactly the same setting. There wasn't one thing different. About 60 or 70 people were there and I was standing at the foot of the grave. I remember, when I positioned myself at the graveside, I was thinking to myself, 'This is exactly where I was standing in my dream!' I couldn't believe it.

As I stood there, when the coffin was being lowered, the exact same thing happened – a blonde girl, who was a friend, walked over and put her arms around me and said, 'You'll be alright, John.' She came over to me at exactly the same time as the coffin was being lowered down. It was precisely the same as in the dream, as if it was set by a clock. She was dressed in black. It was all so precise.

My brother also let off a dove at the graveside. The dove flew upwards and away. As I followed the bird with my eyes I said, 'That's exactly where I was in the dream.' The dove was in the same position as I was while looking down. What I saw was exactly what I would have seen from where the dove was as he flew away. I ask myself, 'How did that happen? What was that about?'

I have had similar dreams over the years. Before I met my wife I had a dream where I was lying down asleep on a couch. I dreamt that a very pretty girl, with long blonde hair, came over to me and kissed me on the forehead. I remember feeling how close she was.

I later met a girl who was exactly the same as the girl in my dream and we got married. At night-time she always goes to bed before me and, when I am lying down on the couch, she leans over and gives me a kiss exactly the same as in the dream.

So these things definitely happen. I put it down to my being a spiritual person. I believe in life after death and that our spirit goes on to another world. I also believe that you have to live a good life to go on and achieve what you hope to get. It's like building a house – if the foundation is bad, the house will come tumbling down. My foundation is to be a spiritual person.

I think that I am tuned in and open to things. I am more sensitive to things like that. I think it's a good thing. I feel we all belong to something that is more powerful than what we are ourselves. But I still don't know the logic behind the dreams and behind what happened in relation to my wife and the death of my mother. I have no explanation. All I know is that they did happen.

JAMES, FROM NORTHERN IRELAND, who described his many premonitions in the previous chapter, has also experienced predictive dreams covering themes including death.

I see many things in my dreams but not all are about death. After one dream I said to my mother-in-law, who lives near us, 'You're going to get a call, in about a year's time, and a neighbour of ours is going to be looking for help with a wee baby that's choking.'

I said, 'You'll be en route, with your son, to the child and I will bump into you on the road. Your son will not be able to take you there because he will have something else important to do. So I'll bring you there and all will be fine.' I could even tell the colours the baby would be wearing.

I forgot all about it and so did my mother-in-law. But, around a year later, I was heading into town with my kids and we met up with her and her son. There was wild panic. I asked her, 'What's up?' She said, 'Do you remember the neighbour you spoke about and her daughter?' I said, 'Yeah.' She said, 'I have to go to her right now, there's a bit of bother.'

She asked me to take her because her son had something else to do. I said, 'Right.'

We went to the house and the woman was there with her baby, who was about six months to a year old. It was the mother's first child. She had put too much clothes on the child and that had caused a fiercely-high temperature. The child was having a kind of fit, like a convulsion. She didn't know what to do. My mother-in-law sorted it all out. As we left the house she said, 'That is weird! That is really, really weird!'

I had another dream, this time about a different neighbour and her death. I dreamt that above her bed was this big bingo ball with the number five on it. It was like one of those big bingo balls that you see on TV but with the number five printed on it. As I looked at the woman on the bed, I knew she wasn't well. But it was the five on the ball that kept grabbing my attention. I couldn't figure out what it meant.

About eight or nine months afterwards the woman became terminally ill. I went to visit her in hospital. She said to me, 'I'm going to pass on.' I knew she was dying. We got on really well and we had a good relationship. I said, 'When you are up with the Big Man, tell him I was asking for him.' She was laughing. She also was thirsty and asked me to get a drink. I gave her milk in a glass through a straw. But I had this bingo ball with the five on my mind and couldn't figure it out.

She eventually died and she was brought from the hospital mortuary to the house. The next day she would normally be brought from the house to the church, with burial on the morning after. But they had to hold off on the burial for two more days because relations had to come from abroad. That was five days! There was a lot of local chat about it. I live in a small community and everyone was saying, 'Imagine they kept her the five days!' I knew then what was meant by the five on the bingo ball.

These inklings of what is coming, or what to do, happen all the time. I could go on and on and on. I don't know why they happen. I know I am more sensitive than most people. You might say I am 'touchy'. But I have had them all my life. They were always there, right from the beginning. It's like an extra sense. Whatever it is, I just live with it.

IT IS WELL ESTABLISHED that the theme of death – as seen in the previous two stories and other narratives in this chapter – often appears in dreams. This is also evident throughout history. Illustrating this point is the following report from the December 1787 edition of *The Scots Magazine*, which features an Irish predictive dream involving death by murder.

One Adam Rogers, a creditable and decent person, a man of good sense and repute, who kept a public house at Portlaw, a small hamlet, nine or ten miles from Waterford, in the kingdom of Ireland, dreamed one night that he saw two men at a particular green spot on the adjoining mountain, one of them a small sickly looking man, the other remarkably strong and large.

He then saw the little man murder the other, and he awoke in great agitation. The circumstances of the dream were so distinct and forcible that he continued much affected by them. He related them to his wife, and also to several neighbours, next morning.

In some time he went out coursing with greyhounds, accompanied, amongst others by one Mr. Browne, the Roman Catholic priest of the parish. He soon stopped at the above-mentioned particular green spot on the mountain, and, calling to Mr. Browne, pointed it out to him, and told him what had appeared in his dream. During the remainder of the day he thought little more about it.

Next morning he was extremely startled at seeing two strangers enter his house, about eleven o'clock in the forenoon. He immediately ran into an inner room, and desired his wife to take particular notice, for they were precisely the two men that he had seen in his dream. When they had consulted with one another, their apprehensions were alarmed for the little weakly man, though contrary to the appearance in the dream.

After the strangers had taken some refreshment, and were about to depart, in order to prosecute their journey, Rogers earnestly endeavoured to dissuade the little man from quitting his house, and going on with his fellow-traveller. He assured him, that if he would remain with him that day, he would accompany him to Carrick the next morning, that being the town to which the travellers were proceeding.

He was unwilling and ashamed to tell the cause of his being so solicitous to separate him from his companion. But, as he observed that Hickey, which was the name of the little man, seemed to be quiet and gentle in his deportment, and had money about him, and that the other had a ferocious bad countenance, the dream still recurred to him. He dreaded that something fatal would happen; and he wished, at all events, to keep them asunder.

However, the humane precautions of Rogers proved ineffectual; for Caulfield, such was the other's name, prevailed upon Hickey to continue with him on their way to Carrick, declaring that, as they had long travelled together, they should not part, but remain together until he should see Hickey safely arrive at the habitation of his friends. The wife of Rogers was much dissatisfied when she found they were gone, and blamed her husband exceedingly for not being absolutely peremptory in detaining Hickey.

About an hour after they left Portlaw, in a lonely part of

the mountain, just near the place observed by Rogers in his dream, Caulfield took the opportunity of murdering his companion. It appeared afterwards, from his own account of the horrid transaction, that, as they were getting over a ditch, he struck Hickey on the back part of his head with a stone; and, when he fell down into the trench, in consequence of the blow, Caulfield gave him several stabs with a knife, and cut his throat so deeply that the head was observed to be almost severed from the body.

He then rifled Hickey's pockets of all the money in them, took part of his clothes, and everything else of value about him, and afterwards proceeded on his way to Carrick. He had not been long gone when the body, still warm, was discovered by some labourers who were returning to their work from dinner.

The report of the murder soon reached to Portlaw. Rogers and his wife went to the place, and instantly knew the body of him whom they had in vain endeavoured to dissuade from going on with his treacherous companion. They at once spoke out their suspicions that the murder was perpetrated by the fellow-traveller of the deceased.

An immediate search was made, and Caulfield was apprehended at Waterford the second day after. He was brought to trial at the ensuing assizes, and convicted of the fact. He walked to the gallows with firm step, and undaunted countenance.

HANORA, FROM COUNTY WATERFORD, had recurring dreams around the time her baby was born. The year was 1976.

I was about seven months pregnant at the time that my recurring dream started. You daren't come home, in those days, if you discovered that you were expecting a baby outside of marriage. If someone did get pregnant they were talked about, read off the altar and snubbed. We got it left, right and centre. We had been told, 'Whatever happens, don't ever get pregnant. And, if you do, don't come running home.'

I was living away from home and I was saying to myself, 'What am I going to do? How am I going to tell my mother?' In two months time I was going to give birth to a baby and I just could not tell her. That was when I started having this recurring dream about my grandmother, who had died when I was eight years old.

My grandmother had been a huge figure in my life up to that. She was part and parcel of every inch of my growing up. She even saved my life when I was a little infant. I was always in tune with her and we got on very well. I always felt she was with me. When I was pregnant I used to ask her, 'What will I do? How will I tell Mam?'

In my recurring dream I was back on the farm where my family lived. There was a very slushy path there, where the cows came into the cow-house. My grandmother was sitting on one side of the path and I was on the other. She was sitting in a chair. I was a little child in this dream and I was asking her to help me across.

I was calling to her and saying, 'Help me across! Help me across!' But she wouldn't help me even though I was crying. She would just sit there and look at me, with a sad kind of a face and her hands on her lap. She would then put her hand up, as if to tell me to go back. It was like a signal saying, 'Stay where you are, you are not coming across!' This recurring dream went on for quite a while.

I used to think about it and say, 'She doesn't want me to tell my mother.' I interpreted it in that way. I found out later that, at the time my grandmother was telling me to go back, my mother was going through a very bad time. Her blood pressure had gone very, very high. She had actually passed out, on one occasion, and broken her wrist. My grandmother would have known that the news that I was pregnant would have killed her.

I had another dream, later on, and my grandmother was again sitting in the chair. She then stood up out of the chair and put her two arms out to me, inviting me to come across that slushy old path where the cows came in. Her arms were outstretched, like she would have done when we were children. I knew she was telling me, 'It's OK now! The coast is clear!' I took it as a sign that the coast was clear to tell my mother.

I found out later on that my mother's blood pressure, by that stage, had been brought under control. She had got medication for it. It was perfect at the time I told her. I think my grandmother was giving me that knowledge. She was looking after her own daughter and also looking after me and my child, all at the same time. I regard what happened as a warning or a prediction. She was telling me what was best to do.

I eventually told my mother about my son, maybe a month before he was born, and I brought him to see her when he was about nine months old. I remember that the day I arrived home was 27 April. My mother stood waiting for me at the door. She took him from me. I said, 'There he is!' He was a beautiful baby.

Then she said, 'My God! I can't believe it. Today would be your sister's birthday had she lived.' We knew we had a sister who had died at birth but we never knew the day or the month. I hadn't known it until then. So that date was always very special to my mother and it became special to me too.

It was, in many ways, the best thing that happened to me. I was terrified of meeting one particular woman where I lived. She was a very old woman. I thought, 'Right! I'll have to face her and she's going to read me the Riot Act and tell me I am a disgrace!' I did face her. I saw her one day. I had my little boy with me and he was about two years of age at the time.

She called me over and said, 'Come in and bring that little fellow with you.' She said, 'I'm glad to see you. How are you?' I thought to myself, 'She's not too bad. I suppose I'll get the brunt of it in a minute.' She then opened a newspaper and said, 'Look at that!' The word 'abortion' was written across the headline. 'Did you go to England and abort that little boy? No, you didn't!' she said. 'You're a great girl and I'm very proud of you!'

What happened is as clear today as it was all those decades ago. I still feel my grandmother around me all the time. Sometimes, when I go to bed, I feel as if there's a little weight on the bed and I know she's there. Often, when I'm alone in the kitchen and washing up, I might feel someone has come into the room. I turn around very quickly and no one is there. But I know she's there. I still feel her around me all the time.

For years I used to wonder what the dream was really all about. I wondered, 'Was it something that I was looking for?' But now I know differently. I think my grandmother, through my dreams, enabled me to tell my mother. And, afterwards, my mother would say to me about my son, 'I've always loved him so much.' I'd say, 'Of course you did, Mam.' And she always brings into it that he came home on my little sister's anniversary. So it was an extremely happy ending.

MARY, FROM COUNTY MEATH, has had prophetic dreams all her life.

I once had a dream about one of my husband's great friends. I remember waking up, one morning, and telling my husband about it. I said, 'I was somewhere in the dream but I can't say where it was. I saw this man and he was in a blue suit in a bed. Everyone was singing around the bed and there was a lot of noise.' I told him I couldn't figure out where I was and I didn't know what was going on or what was happening.

That morning, at nine o'clock, my husband received a phone call to tell him that his great friend had died. When we went up to the house, to the wake, I couldn't believe what I saw. The man was lying in the bed in a blue suit and everybody was sitting around the bed and singing. It clicked immediately. I said, 'My God!' I looked at my husband and said, 'Do you remember, this morning, I was telling you about my dream?' He couldn't believe it.

Another night I had a bad dream about a different friend of my husband's. I recognised him straight away. He used to call to us constantly but we hadn't seen him for two or three weeks. I woke up in the morning and said to my husband, 'I had an awful dream last night. I dreamt I saw your friend in the dream. But he was a terrible colour. He was awfully yellow. He looked dreadful. He didn't look well at all.'

We got word, soon after, that the friend had cancer. Another friend rang and told my husband. I couldn't believe what I was hearing. We went to see the man and he had advanced cancer in the stomach. He looked so yellow. He seemed really sick. I said to my husband, 'I can't believe what I just dreamt of. He looks exactly the same as how he looked in my dream.'

I have had loads of dreams like that. I had some terrible ones when I was much younger but I didn't pay very much attention to them. I never said anything at all about them to anybody. I kept them to myself. I thought they were just things that happened. I thought they happened to everybody else and that was life.

Now, however, when I get up in the morning I try to tell other people about what I saw. I can't wait to ring my daughter and say, 'Do you know what I just dreamt?' If I remember the details, something would always come out of them. I'd suddenly go, 'Gosh! Imagine that has happened! I was only dreaming about it a couple of days ago!'

It's unfortunate that I often forget my dreams. Many times I have dreamt about rivers or water but I would forget about the details by the morning. Other times I am on a plane that will crash and I can hear myself roar and scream. I sometimes get frightened, as a result. But, often, when I try to visualise them they are gone.

I honestly don't know where they come from or what they are. They happen the way they happen. I never take any notice of them. I never think about them. If I dream I dream; if I don't I don't. If a dream is there in the morning, it's there. If it's not there I just let it go. They are just things I see in my sleep. But they are always so real.

JODIE, FROM COUNTY WEXFORD, also recalls forewarnings that have come to her through dreams.

I was in bed, one night, and I had a vivid dream. It happened somewhere between twelve o'clock and half-past-five in the morning. I know because I get up early. In the dream I was in this room. The room wasn't familiar to me. I could see people sitting on chairs all around the walls. I could see them all very clearly. They were sitting on ordinary wooden chairs and there were old black-and-white pictures on the walls.

The people were all relations of my husband. They were men and women. Some of them were still alive, at the time, but others had already died. Some I wouldn't have known that well but others I would. I was naming off all the people I could recognise when, suddenly, I noticed an empty chair. I knew there was somebody missing but I couldn't figure out who it was. It just didn't click with me.

The dream stayed with me the next morning. Then, after lunch, my mother-in-law came down to visit. She lived nearby and wanted to see the baby. I was telling her about the dream. She just said to me, 'That's strange! I wonder who it was that was missing?' Even though I was naming everyone else who was there, she couldn't figure it out either.

A week later she was dead from a heart attack caused by a blood clot. It was only then that I knew. It was like a picture zoomed across my vision and everything slotted into place. I knew it was she was the one that was missing. I could clearly see it was her.

It also was members of her side of the family that I had seen. I was upset at the idea that I had informed her about the dream when I was really telling her that it was she was the one that was missing and going to die.

I had another dream about my mother-in-law. At this stage she was dead. I had been saying to my husband, 'We must get some new net curtains for the windows.' She was saying to me in my dream, 'Don't buy the curtains yet. You're going to get a bargain.'

About a week later I had a letter from my uncle's brother saying that he and his wife were coming over from England on holidays and they asked if they could stay with us. They had stayed with us once before, when I had a cousin who suddenly died. I wrote back and said, 'No problem. That's fine. You're welcome.'

He wrote again and said, 'My wife was shopping and she saw some nice net curtains and they were a really good price. Give us the window measurements and we'll get them for you.' I sent the sizes and they brought me the curtains. I got them for ten pence a yard, which was an amazing bargain. That's another one that came true.

There's a further story, this time concerning my father. I

had a dream about rats and had been told that dreaming of rats can mean a death. I dreamt that the rats were at my father's side of the bed. One rat was lying there and it was like it had been squashed and couldn't breathe. Soon afterwards, on St. Patrick's Day, my father's lung collapsed and he was rushed to hospital. When he was in the hospital I dreamt of rats again. This time they were just lying there on his bed.

He came home, anyway, and I went to see him. He said to me, when I was leaving to go home, 'I'll see you later.' But, at one o'clock on the Tuesday morning, I got a phone call saying he wasn't well. He was taken by ambulance to hospital. We followed the ambulance to the hospital but by the time we got there he had died.

I have regularly had other dreams, involving my grandmother. She's outside her front door in these dreams. The first time this happened she was looking out to the sea, towards the east. Shortly afterwards one of my uncles died in England. The next time this happened she was looking to her right, to the south. Shortly afterwards my own mother died and she lived in that direction.

The third time it happened my grandmother was looking towards the north and my uncle, who lived in that direction, took unwell and ended up in hospital. The final time she was also looking that way and his wife died. It's like as if she is always looking in the direction where something is going to happen.

Some years ago I had another dream, where I was speaking to a man who was on death row. He was waiting to be executed. In the dream he told me his name and he asked me to pray for him. He said his name was Gary and he had murdered some people. He said, 'I'm very sorry for what I've done. I shouldn't have done what I did.' I could see him really clearly and I could see the bars of the cell. He was sitting on the bed while he was telling me this.

In the dream I started saying the Rosary for him. I was talking to him and I felt he was full of remorse. When my husband came in from work, the next day, he handed me the *Evening Herald*. They had a headline about Gary Gilmore and he had been executed the night before. I didn't even know of his existence up to the time of my dream. I also didn't know he was being executed.

I have had loads more dreams. They have happened a lot. Sometimes they worry me and I wonder about them. They can give me a fright. I get frightened especially when they come true. I don't tell too many people, as a result. They might think I'm a bit weird.

I have no control over the dreams. During some nights they happen; other nights I don't dream at all. Sometimes they are ordinary, everyday dreams. I also have others that I don't understand at the time. Sometimes I remember them; other times I mightn't remember them but they will come straight back to me after something happens. They can be a bit weird. But I don't think of it as a gift. It's just something that happens.

OTHER PRESENTIMENTS

In 1921 James Chaffin, a farmer from North Carolina, USA, died from a fall leaving his wife and four sons behind. That year was a tough one in America, characterised by high unemployment, plummeting stock prices and company failures. It became even tougher for Chaffin's wife and three of his sons when it was discovered that Mr. Chaffin had made a will in 1905 leaving all his possessions to one son while making no provision for the rest of the family.

Although the will was duly executed, the story didn't end there. In 1925, four years after Chaffin's death, one of his disinherited sons – also called James – described how he was twice visited by his deceased father while on the edge of sleep. During the first visit the father said nothing. During the second visit, however, he opened the coat he was wearing and indicated inside. He instructed his son, 'You will find my will in my overcoat pocket.'

James Junior travelled the following day to his mother's home, where he discovered that his father's overcoat had been given to his brother John. On arrival at John's house, he opened the coat and discovered a rather strange note from his father. It was hidden in the inside pocket, which had been stitched shut. The note simply said, 'Read the twenty-seventh chapter of Genesis in my daddy's old Bible.'

Having located the Bible – and in the presence of witnesses, including his mother, his daughter and a neighbour – it was found to contain a replacement will in a folded page in

Genesis 27. The will, written in 1919, ordered the division of the family's property between all four sons and charged them to take care of their mother.

Although legally contested in court, the will was adjudged to be authentic. In its decision the court was swayed by the evidence of ten witnesses who testified that the father's handwriting was genuine. The old will was summarily annulled and the new one probated. With that one of the most extraordinary cases in American legal history came to a close, with the division of family property ultimately being decided by an intervention from beyond the grave.

Throughout the course of my research for this book, I have encountered many similar stories of strange forewarnings that surfaced in the most peculiar ways. These stories are featured in this chapter. One involves a deceased relative who is said to have returned with information regarding a future death.

Other stories involve people who, while at the edge of death, have appeared to those who are close to them. An additional story recounts a sense of déjà vu, where it was perceived that a situation had been seen or experienced at an earlier time.

Further events are recalled where strange lights, auras or noises turned out to be harbingers of death. These noises often involve crystal-clear 'knocking' sounds on doors or on windows, which are widely credited as being bad omens in many parts of the country. Another story relates how a mechanical device stopped at the precise time that a family member died.

There are also narratives involving the unusual and unexpected appearance of particular species of birds at the time of death. The unfortunate robin is often believed to be a death omen should it either knock on a window or appear in a house. Black birds, such as crows and ravens, are likewise taken to be portents of doom. This legend has occasionally been broadened to include the blackbird, which is better known for its melodious singing.

The vast majority of these stories have death as a common denominator. All 18 case histories featured below involve the passing away of parents, children, spouses, relatives, work colleagues, close friends or distant acquaintances. It is intriguing, indeed, that so many death narratives should dominate the following pages.

ERNEST, FROM DUBLIN, describes the strange thing that happened at the precise time his brother tragically died.

I had a watch, for many years, which was bought for me by my father. It's a gold wristwatch and it was the first watch I ever had. My dad gave it to me over ten years ago at least. It has a black square face on it. But it got worn out over time. It got badly beaten. You have to be careful of it or the strap will fall apart.

I had a brother who was 11 years older than me. We were best friends and very close. We could have been twins, except for the age gap. We were very alike, the spitting image of each other. We had similar personalities. We were into the same things and liked the same films and music. Both of us were also big fans of boxing and wrestling.

When I was young I did a bit of boxing. My brother would occasionally do a bit of sparring with me. One day we were training together, doing a bit of messing around in his house. I was wearing my watch and the strap was broken on it. It was very stupid of me to be wearing it. I cut his arm, by accident, and left him with a bit of a mark.

He said to me, 'Would you ever get rid of that watch!' I said, 'No, no, no, I'm going to keep it.' He was always on at me, trying to get me to get rid of it. He would say, 'Try and get something better. It doesn't look too well. I'll get you a new one.' But I liked it and I said to him, 'No. I will keep it.' It meant a lot to me. So he would say, 'I'll get rid of it for you!'

I had been with him four days before he died. I spent the whole day with him. We had a cup of coffee together and something to eat. That evening I went up to his house and helped him do some things. It was strange because he seemed to be getting everything in order. He was putting things up in the attic. I was helping him.

Sometime beforehand he had decided, all of a sudden, to decorate the whole house. The things he was doing were out of character. When I look back at it, what he was doing was getting things ready. That last day I also met him for about half an hour. He was on at me again over the watch. He said, 'I'll get rid of it for you, don't worry!'

That night my brother was tragically killed doing his job as a security man. He died and the watch stopped at exactly the time he was killed. It stopped at eight-minutes-to-eleven. I discovered it the next morning. I checked with the police to find out the time he died. It all just came together. I knew it. It all made sense. It hasn't moved ever since.

What happened badly affected me. I have been bothered over the years. I've seen things and gone through things that someone as young as me shouldn't have gone through. I have had numerous dreams about him. In one dream he is on a train. I always ask him the same question, 'Where have you been?' He gives me the same answer, 'I am around.' He then disappears.

In another dream he comes to me while I'm outside a church. It's the church he was christened in and had his communion and confirmation in. He comes up to me and asks me to help him. I wouldn't know what he's talking about. Then he'd say to me, 'Someone is going to get me!' I'd say, 'Who's going to get you?' He'd say, 'Come on, I'll show you!' So we go inside the church and inside would be two men attacking my brother. He'd ask me to help him. I'd stand right in front of him, to help him. But the two men would disappear and I'd wake up.

The only thing that gives me comfort is that I was the last person he was with before he died. Of all the people he could have been with, I'm glad it was me. It's like as if it was some kind of last moment. I still feel that he is with me. I even felt he was in my room one night. With little things like that happening, I feel him around me all the time.

I still have the watch, although I don't wear it. It's back in its original box and it's up in my wardrobe. When I look at it now, I see sadness in it. I don't pick up a pleasant feeling from it. I know I could try and put a battery in it to see if it would work. But I don't want to touch it.

I will never get rid of it. I will always believe it was my brother who came to me and who stopped it. I think he would have thought it was funny. He was quite a character. He would have been quite pleased to think that he had the last laugh.

BRIGID, FROM COUNTY LOUTH, had a most disturbing forewarning of a work colleague's death.

I was training as a nurse in Manchester, back in the late 1950s. One day I was in the dining-room, which held about 100 nurses sitting at wooden tables. There would be six at a table. The food would be put out and you just sat there and ate. There would also be a lot of chatter about what was happening in the wards.

This day, to my left, I could see various nurses coming through the door. I suddenly saw two girls coming in. Both were Irish. When I looked I could see what was like an

155

archway of fog, containing black spots, around the younger of the two girls. The fog was grey-coloured. It was a bit like a grey cloud of cotton wool but it didn't actually touch her. It extended about 18 inches out from her body and stretched all around her, up around her head to a height of well over five feet.

I had never seen anything like it before. It certainly wasn't sunlight. The end of the dining-room was dark and she was framed not by a window but by the wall behind her. It also wasn't the lighting in the dining-room. It was just there and I was shocked to see it. It wasn't a pretty sight or a nice image. It was like something out of this world and it scared me and alarmed me.

I turned and pointed her out to the other girls at the table. I asked them, 'What is that around her?' They all looked and couldn't see anything. My friend, who also came from County Louth, put on her glasses and looked. She said, 'Sorry, there's nothing there.' When I glanced back again the fog and the spots were gone.

The other nurses started making fun of me. I was annoyed. I got up and walked out and went up to my room. I remember my friend came up to me later on. I said, 'I'm not really pleased with any of you.' She asked me again, 'What exactly did you see?' I said, 'I told you already.' I wouldn't repeat it.

The next morning I went down to the dining-room for breakfast. There were about 20 or 30 nurses there. There wasn't a sound at the tables. Nobody was talking. It was very unusual. On my way in I said to one of the maids, 'What's wrong? There is not a sound. Why is everything so quiet?' She said, 'It's because of that nurse.' I said, 'What nurse?' She said, 'The one in the accident last night, the nurse that was killed.'

I asked her, 'What are you talking about?' She said, 'Didn't you hear?' She didn't know the name of the nurse but she told me again that one of them had been killed. I immediately went down to the tables. It was there that I heard that the nurse who was killed was the one around whom I had seen the fog and spots the previous day.

It turned out that she and a friend had been at the Irish Club in Manchester the night before. They went by bus. The bus would take you there and bring you back and drop you outside the hospital gates. The two of them arrived back at about 11 o'clock. Once they got off the bus they walked from behind it straight out onto the road.

The nurse who was killed unfortunately went under a car. She couldn't hear it coming because of the roar of the bus. She was killed instantly. The other girl was pushed up against the bus and was three months in hospital. She was lucky that she lived. I ended up nursing her at one stage.

I said to the others at the table, after they told me who was killed, 'That was the girl I was talking about yesterday, the girl that I saw the fog around.' They couldn't believe what had happened. They were amazed and were questioning me about what I saw. I felt they were almost accusing me of killing her.

They said, 'Sorry we made fun of you.' Someone also said to me, 'Why didn't you tell her?' But what could I tell her, that there was an archway of fog around her? The girl would probably have laughed at me. One of them said, 'You must be psychic.' I don't think I had even heard the word 'psychic' at the time.

I rang home to my mother and I told her what had happened. She had seen things like that over the years. My mother's aunt had experienced things like that as well. So has my daughter. It's all on my mother's side. It seems to have come down through the female side but I don't know how or why.

I can't even properly explain to myself what happened. I think it was a forewarning and a sign of death. I knew that I had seen something that wasn't really of this world. I knew it was something from another dimension. That's the only way I can explain it. And I knew it wasn't good.

I don't speak about it because a lot of people would say, 'It's a fairytale.' But it's not. I know I saw something that others couldn't see. One second it was there; the next time I looked it was gone. It happened so quickly. But I have no doubt that it happened and I definitely know there was a connection between what I saw and what took place that night.

MARY, FROM CORK, also had an advance warning of a death – this time the death of her daughter. It happened in 1991.

My daughter was aged 18 in 1991. She was studying for her Leaving Cert. at the time. She was a half-twin and full of life. I would say to her, 'Can't you calm down?' She would say to me, 'Mam, you're only young once.' She loved style and glamour. All she wanted to do was travel but she never got a chance.

In early 1991 I was in bed one night. All the family were in bed, asleep. I woke suddenly, in the middle of the night, and I saw my daughter standing at the bedroom door. I always leave the bedroom door open. But it wasn't actually my daughter who was there. She was in bed, asleep. What I saw was more like an apparition. It was just like herself standing at the door, although it wasn't her.

My daughter was dressed in a black polo-neck. All I was really focused on was the polo-neck. That's the only thing that stood out. Everything else about her was the same. I got a fright when I saw her but I just thought it was a dream and I turned over towards the wall and went back to sleep.

A short time later I met up with a friend of mine. She used to borrow my daughter's clothes. I met her at mass and she asked me if my daughter had got any new clothes. I said, 'Come up and have a look.' She did. She came to the house.

When she came up to my bedroom she noticed that my bed is up against the wall. She said to me, 'I don't know how you can sleep with your bed like that. I have to have mine in the middle of the floor.' I said, 'I was very glad of that the other night because I saw an apparition of my daughter at the door. I got an awful fright. When I saw her I turned into the wall and thought no more of it.' I told her all about what had happened and what I had seen.

Sometime afterwards I went out with my sister for a drink. My daughter was at home, studying for her Leaving Cert. I asked her if she was meeting her boyfriend that night. She told me she wasn't. She was going out with a boyfriend who had a bike. Anytime he came for her I used always say, 'Don't get up on that motorbike!' I dreaded it. I asked her, 'Is it all off?' She said, 'No. I'm meeting him tomorrow night.' So I went off with my sister for the drink.

We were having our drink when an announcement came over the loudspeaker. It said that I was wanted on the telephone. I went out and, as I did, there was a man coming in who said, 'I'm just after coming across a terrible motorbike accident. I'm sure the two of them are dead.' I never even spoke to the person on the phone. I just dropped it and I came back in and said to my sister, 'I'm sure my daughter is dead!' She thought I was going crazy.

There was a Guard there that night. He came over to me and he asked me if I was alright. I explained to him what I thought. He got on the phone but he wouldn't tell me what he learned. I insisted that I wouldn't go home and the Guard brought me to the hospital. The priest who was there told me that my daughter had died. It was then that the Guard told me that if I wanted to see her I would have to go to the morgue. When I arrived my daughter's body was there, on a pull-out bed.

I was devastated. She hadn't a mark on her. But the strange thing was that she was dressed in the same black polo-neck that I saw her in at my bedroom door. I didn't think about the black polo-neck until afterwards. I don't remember how long it was before I established the connection and remembered the image of her standing there. But what I saw in the morgue was identical to what I had seen that night from my bed.

It turned out that my daughter's boyfriend had come down and collected her sometime after I left. About ten minutes from the house he crashed into a telegraph pole and the two of them were killed instantly. I was distraught. She was so healthy and you don't expect death. I never got over it. I just live with it but I'll never forget it.

Another strange thing about it happened later when I went to the priest to get a mass said for my daughter's anniversary. I asked him to say the mass in May, when she had died. He said, 'May is all booked out.' He asked me the date. I said it was 12 May. He said, 'That's strange, that's the only day that's available.' So he put me down for the mass.

Later, when her twin was getting married, I had to go to the same priest to get her baptism cert. It turned out that they had both been baptised on 12 May. The date she had died was the same date she was baptised. The priest, when he saw it, said the hairs stood up on the back of his neck.

Looking back at the apparition, I just don't know what it was. It was definitely a very strange connection, some sort of forewarning. But it wasn't what I expected. I certainly didn't expect to see my daughter dead in the sweater. But that's the way it happened. And at least I told my friend what I had seen that night from my bed. Otherwise, nobody would have believed me when I told them what had happened.

JOHNNY, WHO COMES ORIGINALLY FROM DUBLIN **but who now lives in County Mayo, had a strange experience on the night an old friend passed away.**

There was a woman who was a very close friend of ours and who lived near us in Dublin. She was a very sweet lady, a very angelic woman, and was very fond of me. She was like my second mother. She had a constant smile on her face and you would never hear her complaining. It was rare to meet someone like her.

Because she had a huge family, she was constantly at the cooker. She was always concerned about all her lads, even though they were in their 40s and 50s. She was also well-known throughout the area. Lads would drop in to her for a bit of soup after a few pints.

The time came when she was very sick and she had to be hospitalised. At this stage she was in her 70s. I was living and working in County Mayo and I wasn't able to get to see her. Over the years I had gone up to visit but while she was sick we hadn't met.

I was living in a flat at the time. One night I was with my flatmate. It was after ten o'clock. I was watching TV in the sitting-room. I got extremely drowsy and felt very weak. I said to my flatmate, 'I'm just going to lie down.' I went to the bedroom and lay on the bed. I was so weak it felt like the life was going out of my body. It almost felt like I was fainting. I didn't fall asleep but my body felt lifeless.

The woman's face suddenly came into my mind and I felt I was talking to her. I could see her face and I could hear her voice. We had a conversation. She was worried about her lads. She was saying, 'How will they cope without me?' I was telling her not to worry about them, they'd be fine. I was saying, 'You have done enough. You have been standing by the cooker all your life. They are old enough to look after themselves.' I then said, 'You've got to go. Have a rest for yourself.'

It was as if I was having a conversation with her. It was also as if I was telling her to let go and that she could pass on. I had no fear and wasn't surprised or frightened. This whole thing lasted about ten or fifteen minutes. I then came out of it and felt life coming back into my body. I felt quite normal again. But I felt very sad because I knew it was time for her to go.

I went back into the sitting-room. I said to my flatmate, 'What time is it?' He said, 'It's twenty-to-eleven.' I said, 'Remember that time!' He said, 'Why?' I asked him again to remember it and he said he would. I suppose I wanted him to remember the time as proof for myself that my imagination wasn't playing tricks with me. I was thinking that something had happened, that she had listened to me and was going to pass over. I knew there was something to it.

The next morning her family rang me and told me she had died the night before. I asked the woman's daughter, 'What time did it happen? What time did she die?' She said, 'It was just after twenty-to-eleven last night.' I then explained to my flatmate why I had asked him to remember the time and he was flabbergasted. He was my proof that the thing did happen.

I think that what had happened involved telepathy or a message or something like that. I can't think of an appropriate word. I think some people are more open to accepting these messages than others. Other people block them and don't let them in. If you allow yourself, and you are not afraid, then you can receive them.

I think she was communicating with me as she was passing away. It was nice that she wanted to do that. I guess she was somewhere on the edge of unconsciousness and had to choose what she was going to do. She had to decide whether she was staying or passing on. So I'm glad I got to talk to her. She needed the encouragement to pass over. She was weak and sick and it was her time to go.

TONY, FROM CORK CITY, describes how his deceased grandmother forewarned him that his uncle was dying. The event happened around a decade ago.

One night I was in bed and my grandmother appeared to me. It was about half-past-three in the morning. I was fast asleep. I suddenly sat up and there she was, at the foot of the bed. She was dressed in a Child of Mary blue smock and was wearing a medal as well. She had a brooch on, with a lady's head in it, and a Rosary beads in her hand. She was a good-looking woman, with a plump face, and she had white hair tied up in a bun at the back.

She was crystal clear, as if it was her real self in front of me. She was telling me something but I couldn't make out what she was saying. I woke my wife up and told her about it. I said, 'I think there's something wrong at home!' My wife said, 'You can't ring home at this hour.'

I knew that my mother got up early, at around seven o'clock or so. I said, 'I'll wait until then and I'll ring.' I rang at seven o'clock but I couldn't get through. I was panicking. I did eventually get through and the first thing I asked my mother was, 'Are things alright at home?' She said, 'Oh, they're alright at home. But your uncle is dying in hospital and he's looking for you.'

I got into the car and shot up to the hospital. I got there at about twenty-past-seven. My uncle, who I was exceptionally close to, knew me straight away and caught my hand and greeted me. He had taken me to hurling matches and football matches and bought me my first hurley when I was young. We were very close. I was glad I was there because he soon went into a coma and he left us at around a quarter-to-eight. He died peacefully.

I told my mother what had happened. She was dismissive at first. But when I described my grandmother in detail, my mother turned snow-white. You must remember that I hadn't known my grandmother. I was three years of age when she died. My mother then told me that my grandmother had been buried in a Child of Mary blue smock and medal and she also wore a brooch with a lady's head in it. She had a Rosary beads in her hand.

I believe that I experienced a forewarning, no doubt about that. I've said it to one or two people and they have been a bit sheepish about it. I think, in modern life, we have lost our belief in things like that. But I know it happened. I think my grandmother came to me to warn me that my uncle was dying and that he was looking for me to say goodbye.

COLETTE, FROM COUNTY DONEGAL, describes the curious events surrounding the death of her father.

What happened dates back to the weekend of the All-Ireland final in 1992, which was won by Donegal. I wanted to go up to Dublin for the match but I couldn't because my father was coming to stay. He was 72 years of age and was living in County Tyrone. He decided to come to me for the weekend, just for a visit.

He had arrived on the Friday and on the Saturday we got up as normal. I remember it was a nice day in September. I thought he was in good health. There was no big illness. He was always complaining, down through the years, but there was nothing apparently wrong at the time.

At about three o'clock in the afternoon, I decided to sweep the outside of the house. My dad was lying on the settee in the sitting-room, just inside a large front window. All his life he had a habit of lying down. He wouldn't be reading papers; he would just be dozing. There was nothing unusual about it. He was inside the window and I was sweeping outside.

About ten yards down from me was the entrance to the house. There are two white cement pillars there, with black gates. I suddenly saw my father crossing the entryway. He was crossing between the two pillars, walking from pillar to pillar along the road. He was wearing grey clothes, like a jumper and trousers. He had grey hair. I picked him out immediately as my father. It was definitely him.

I thought he had gone out the back door. I said, 'He must be going over to the neighbour's house.' Where I lived was remote. There were no other people around. There was also no possible way it could have been anybody else because there was nobody else about. It never occurred to me to shout at him because I knew it was him. I didn't even think that it could have been anybody else.

I went in home immediately afterwards. I came into the sitting-room and there he was lying on the settee. I was standing at the door of the sitting-room. I got a start. I said to him, 'Daddy, I saw you outside. I thought you were going over to the neighbour's.' He said, 'Oh, no! I wasn't outside! It was my ghost!' He was quite calm and realistic about it. What I said seemed to be confirming to him that he was going to die.

That weekend he burned all of his stuff that he had in Donegal. Then, on the Monday morning, as we were leaving the house and going out through the gates, he started to cry. I said, 'Daddy, what's wrong with you?' He said, 'I won't see this place again!' I asked him, 'What makes you think that?' All his people had lived until they were very old. As a joke I said, 'They had to be shot!' He said, 'I hope you are right but I don't think so.'

Within three weeks my father was dead. I had forgotten about what had happened and had got on with things. It had gone out of my head. But, one night, about three weeks after his visit, I got a phone call to ask if we could all go to the hospital in Omagh. I was told he was very ill. I went there. He had a heart attack and he died having never come back to the house.

My mother had the same sort of experience with her father. This was back in the late 1950s, before the phone age. He was in hospital, in Donegal town, and she was coming down to ask how he was in the morning. On her way she saw him walking down by the river. She thought, 'Oh, he's home!' But he wasn't home. He died soon afterwards.

I've had loads of other experiences. In January 1978 I got a premonition that my mother was going to die. I just got this strong feeling. It came out of nowhere. I cried all night and in the morning my mother said, 'Why are your eyes red?' I said, 'It's nothing at all. I'm OK.' My sister was living at home and her husband was away at the time. I told her what had happened but I thought no more about it. Within nine months my mother was buried.

More recently my aunt died in Wales. The evening before she died I was in the garden picking up stones. I heard three massive wails. I looked everywhere. But, as I said, there's really nobody living around me. A lot of the houses are empty because of emigration. That night I was in bed and I got a phone call from another aunt to tell me that my aunt in Wales had taken very ill and had been brought to hospital. She died soon after.

I think I have some kind of 'second sight' that warns me of these things. I am tuned in to them. I think a lot and I am probably very sensitive. I would also be a sort of nervous person. I have lived alone and I have had a very difficult life. I have suffered quite a lot and maybe that has something to do with it.

I was also brought up in an era, and in an area of the country, where we were more receptive to things like that. Whatever they are I am sure they are real. I couldn't make them up even though I have a good imagination. There's also far too many of them. I think they are really premonitions or forewarnings of what's to come and I have definitely experienced them.

MARIAN, FROM COUNTY CORK, remembers the events that took place on the day her mother died. The date was 1 August 1986.

I was living in America, in Michigan, at the time. They call it 'God's Country'. It is absolutely beautiful. I lived right on Lake Michigan and had been there for about two years. The night of 31 July we all went to bed as usual. I had a little boy of my own. There also was a little girl who had come up for a week during the summer to stay with me and to be with my little son. My husband wasn't there because he worked nights. I went to bed probably around 11 o'clock.

Early in the morning I woke up. I looked at the clock and it said 2.30. I could hear this loud ticking. It was constant ticking, like the loud ticking of a clock. But I had no clocks that ticked. They were all silent, battery-powered clocks. The ticking was just loud enough to wake me up and make me aware that something was after happening. I thought, 'What's going on?'

The ticking didn't last that long, just enough to make me sit up in the bed and wonder, 'Where is the noise coming from?' What immediately came into my mind was something my mother used to say to us when we were children growing up. She said, 'When somebody very close to you dies, you hear a loud ticking.' I remember her telling that to my sisters and I when we were small.

We grew up in the olden times, in County Cork. I think what my mother had meant was, 'If you aren't there when somebody you love dies – if you are far away – a loud ticking noise will tell you.' So I knew instantly that something had happened. I said, 'Oh, God! Somebody's dead!' I just knew it. When I realised that, the ticking stopped.

At that moment I could feel somebody in the room with me. I couldn't see anything but I could feel a presence. I thought, 'Mam, is that you?' I remember saying it. Everything felt so lovely and warm, and I wasn't afraid. I was so sure it was my mother that I went into the nursery, right off my bedroom, and showed her my little son.

I literally walked around the house showing her the rooms. What I did didn't seem one bit strange, even though I'm the sort of person who would be scared of my own shadow. I was just happy walking around with her. I even made tea. I just knew it was my mother and why would I be afraid of her?

Twenty minutes later, at 2.50, my phone rang. I picked it up. It was my dad. I said, 'It is Mam, isn't it?' I knew he was going to tell me about my mother. He said, 'How do you know?' I said, 'She's here with me.' I started crying and I knew then that she was gone. I was devastated because I loved her so much.

My dad then told me what had happened. The weird thing

about it was that my mam had died at 7.30 in the morning, Irish time. At the time we had a five-hour difference between Ireland and Michigan. When I woke up it was 2.30 and she died at 7.30, Irish time. The very minute she passed away, I woke up.

I returned to Ireland immediately. When I came back home I heard what had happened. My mam had been up at mass for the First Friday. She always made the First Friday mornings. At that time they heard the First Friday mass in the hallway of the local cottage hospital. They had the altar just inside the door and they had chairs in the hallway. My mother was speaking to a nurse, sitting down and chatting. The nurse told me, 'I thought she had fainted but she just dropped dead.' She was only 65 years of age.

Nothing like that has ever happened to me before or since. That was the only time I heard that ticking in my life. The explanation, I think, is that my mother loved me so much that she came to me. I was in America, on my own, and the rest of my family was in Ireland.

I know she missed me. I know I was important to her. I also know she wanted to see my house. She had always wanted to come to visit me but she never had because my dad was a sort of a home bird. I think she came to me that night, at the time she died, just to see me, to see my house and to see my little son.

I can't think of any other explanation. I lived out in the country, in north Michigan. It was a beautiful area. There were a few little houses around but it wasn't like I was in a town, with streets and cars and lights that could have woken me up. If anything could have woken me up, it would have been the child. But that didn't happen. The only thing that woke me up was the ticking.

I feel that something special happened that night. Why else

would I have woken up at 2.30 in the morning? Why else would I have heard a loud ticking especially when I had no clock that ticked? Why else would I have felt the presence of my mother? And how could I tell my father that I knew? She had to have come to me. Something special had to have happened that night. I know it did.

BRENDAN, FROM COUNTY KERRY, experienced an unsettling warning of a friend's forthcoming death.

One Sunday I was at mass. I was sitting there waiting for the mass to begin. I saw a friend's family over at another section of the church, at the other side of the altar away from me. There was his mother and son and wife and sister. They all came in at different intervals and joined each other in the same seat. They sat in a particular sequence. But my friend wasn't there. He used to go to mass during the week but never on a Sunday.

The one thing that was striking, and why I noticed them, was that they were all wearing white coats except for my friend's wife who was wearing a dark purple coat. It was because of the coats that they stood out in my mind. There was something I sensed about what I was seeing. Something struck me. I mentioned it to my aunt later on that day. I told her I saw the family there and told her about the coats. And that was the end of that.

What had happened would mean nothing normally, but a month or six weeks later my friend died suddenly. He hadn't been sick. He just died in his sleep and was buried soon after. Then there was a 'month's mind'. I went along to it and was sitting down. I looked over and noticed all his family again.

All the same family members were there, all wearing the white coats except for his wife who was wearing a black coat. It was the exact same people, in the exact same sequence they had been in six weeks previously. Everything was precisely the same.

It probably means nothing at all but, to me, it was as if a repeat of the event had taken place. I just don't understand its significance. But I wonder, 'Why did I notice it in the first place?' It certainly did register and I did mention it to my aunt when it happened first. It certainly struck me that something was strange.

I also told my aunt about it when I came home from the 'month's mind'. I told her how the family were all in the same coats and in the same sequence. She felt there was something to it that was stronger than coincidence, although she couldn't explain it. I also feel there was something to it, although I can't explain it either.

FRANK, WHO COMES ORIGINALLY FROM COUNTY LONGFORD, can foresee other people's deaths. He developed this ability following a near-death experience back in the 1960s.

The first one happened in 1979. I was working in a factory at the time. One day I was with a friend of mine and we were bringing parts down to the main floor. We bumped into my friend's friend. Whenever it used to happen they always had chats about football, although I had no interest in football and never did. One of them was mad into Manchester United; the other was into Liverpool. That's how the conversation went.

I was standing there waiting for the conversation to finish. I was facing my friend's friend. Whatever way I looked at him, the pupils of his eyes turned black. They went marble black. I couldn't believe what I was seeing. I turned to my friend but he was talking away. I couldn't believe that he wasn't seeing what I was seeing, especially as they were face-to-face.

I then looked to the other guy and the eyeballs of his eyes were so black that I could see the reflection of myself, upside down, in them. It was really pronounced. It was weird. I felt alarmed and I couldn't believe what was happening.

I looked back at my friend, once more, but he was still talking away. I still couldn't believe he wasn't seeing the same thing. When I turned back to the other guy, his eyes were blue again. The conversation finished, soon after, and my friend and I went on our way.

I said to him, 'Did you notice anything strange about your friend?' 'Like what?' he said. I said, 'The pupils of his eyes turned black!' He was incredulous. I told him what I saw, that the pupils had turned black. I'm sure he thought I was talking rubbish. But I knew I had seen it and I knew there was nothing wrong with me.

I went home that evening and said it to my wife. She said, 'You are imagining things.' I went into work the following morning. My friend and I were there at five-to-eight. Another person came in and said to my friend, 'I have bad news for you.' He told him that the other guy – the one we had been talking to – had killed himself the previous night. He had committed suicide. My friend turned to me and said, 'What did you say to me yesterday?'

It has happened four times since. One of them occurred around 1995. It was the August Bank Holiday weekend. My wife and I had gone back to where I had grown up, to see my mother. We stayed the weekend. My wife saw a top that she liked in the window of a clothes shop. On the Monday she wanted me to stop and have a look at it to see what I thought. We got out of the car and we were walking down towards the shop when we met an ex-neighbour of mine.

The exact same thing happened. It wasn't as pronounced as the first time. We had our backs to the sun and he was facing the sun. I later said it to my wife and she said, 'You are imagining it.' We came home that evening. We were back about an hour when my mother phoned and said, 'You know our neighbour?' and she mentioned his name. I said, 'Yeah.' She said, 'He was killed in a car crash, on the Dublin road, about a half-an-hour ago.' That was only about three or four hours after I had seen him.

The last time it happened was in 2010. I was in a pub, one night, and I saw this woman sitting there with a man. There was myself, another man and this couple in the pub. I was on my way elsewhere and I just dropped in for a pint. When I sat down I looked over at the woman, who was a good bit away from me. The first thing that crossed my mind was, 'That woman's mascara is after running all over her face.' Her eyes were all black. It was like she had two big black eyes.

I thought I should tell her. As I got to the end of my pint, I got up to let her know. But, just as I walked towards her, she got up and the two of them left. The following day I was telling my wife what happened. I then forgot all about her. Two weeks later I saw that she had been murdered. I was watching TV and there was her face on the screen.

Overall it has happened on five occasions. One of the events involved my mother. She was admittedly in a nursing home and she was 84 at the time. But, one day, when I went up to see her, the first thing I noticed was that her eyes were marble black. She passed away that night.

It hasn't happened a lot and I don't like it happening. But I believe it goes back to a near-death or after-death experience I had when I was 14 and I nearly drowned. I'm convinced of that. I don't know the connection. I often thought of getting hypnotised, to bring me back to what happened when I was young and to relive it. But I haven't done it. It remains a mystery to me, in the meantime, and I don't know where it comes from.

THE FOLLOWING DESCRIBES a forewarning of another person's death, which took place in 1888. This story was recorded in the book *Psychical Research*, which was written by the Dublin-based Professor of Physics Sir William Barrett and first published in 1911.

In the following case a note of the apparition seen shortly before death was made at the time, and preserved by the percipient, when she had no knowledge of the brief, fatal illness of the deceased.

The percipient, Miss Hervey, then staying in Tasmania with Lady H., had just come in from a ride in excellent health and spirits, and was leaving her room upstairs to have tea with Lady H., when she saw coming up the stairs the figure of her cousin, a nurse in Dublin, to whom she was much attached.

She at once recognised the figure, which was dressed in grey, and without waiting to see it disappear, she hurried to Lady H., whom she told what she had seen. Lady H. laughed at her, but told her to note it down in her diary, which she did.

Diary and note were seen by the critical Mr. Podmore, who investigated the case on behalf of the S.P.R. (Society For Psychical Research). The note ran as follows: 'Saturday, April 21, 1888, 6 p.m. Vision of (giving her cousin's nickname) on landing in grey dress.'

In June news of this cousin's unexpected death reached Miss Hervey in Tasmania. She died in a Dublin hospital from typhus fever on April 22, 1888. A letter, written the same day, giving an account of Miss Ethel B.'s death, was sent to Miss Hervey, preserved by her, and seen by Mr. Podmore.

It states that the crisis of the illness began at 4 a.m. on the 22nd, but that Miss B. lingered on for twelve hours, dying at

4.30 p.m. As the difference of time between Tasmania and Dublin is about ten hours, the apparition preceded the actual death by some thirty-two hours.

The kind of dress worn by the nurses in the hospital was unknown to Miss Hervey, and was found to be of a greyish tone when seen from a little distance.

The phantom made so vivid an impression on Miss Hervey that, on the evening she saw it, she wrote a long letter to her cousin in Dublin telling her about it. This letter arrived some six weeks after her death, and was returned to the writer.

KATHLEEN, FROM COUNTY KERRY, **recalls how appearances from robins are often connected to deaths in her family. The first event she recounts dates back to the end of 1973.**

It was shortly after Christmas in 1973. We were all sitting around the dining-room table at home in Kerry. There were around six of us there including my sister, mother and father and an aunt. We were just chatting and maybe having a drink or a cup of tea, around ten o'clock. I remember it was a really dark winter's night.

We were deep in conversation when, suddenly, there was a loud knock on the back door. We were chatting and the TV was probably on, yet we all heard it. My mother went and opened the door. A robin flew past her into the house. For a little bird to make such a knock was incredible. I can remember my mother said either, 'Oh, a messenger!' or 'Oh, *the* messenger!' Nobody else said anything but I think her reaction got me all bothered. We opened windows and got the robin out.

I think my father was the first to go to bed. Afterwards my sister and I quizzed my mother about what had happened. We were saying that we didn't like the idea of it. I had it in my head that it wasn't lucky to have a robin come into a house. I suppose the word 'lucky' was a euphemism for something more sinister, some sort of ominous forewarning. I thought it was a bad sign.

I really don't know where my fear came from. It was some sort of family tradition. But my mother played it down by saying, 'Oh! For heaven's sake! Don't be ridiculous! There are lots of robins around!' She calmed us down. And that was the end of that, although I still wasn't happy after what had happened. It hung over me afterwards and I thought about it several times.

About seven weeks later, in February, my father died. He was out for a walk and he got a massive heart attack. He was only 64 and, although he had a heart problem about ten years earlier, he was in good health at the time. He had been minding himself and his death was totally unexpected.

I was living and working in Dublin. I remember well it was the year of the petrol crisis – 1974 – and we had to siphon petrol out of cars to get down from Dublin to Kerry. I will never forget it. But I will also never forget his death coming so soon after the appearance of the robin.

My mother died ten years later, back in 1984. She died in Dublin, where she had been sick and in hospital. This time a neighbour told us that there had been a dead robin outside the house in Kerry on the day she died. He told me this after my mother was buried. He said, 'I went down to your house, on the day your mother died, and a dead robin was lying under the window.' He must have known about our family and robins.

The net result is that I now never send Christmas cards with images of robins on them. I have a little thing about that. I take them out of packets and get rid of them. I did it once, I think, and I shouldn't have. I was stuck for a card and I think it went off to America. But I didn't want to send it. Thank God, nothing happened. I don't mind getting them because the people who send them to me don't know. But I certainly wouldn't send them myself.

I suppose it's some sort of tradition which I inherited. I must have heard it at a very young age and it buried itself in my subconscious. I obviously got it from my mother, who was very sensitive. I think it might have followed her side of the family, like some sort of folklore.

You hear about all of these things, like omens, that follow certain families. Sometimes they are flashes of light or hares or magpies or, of course, robins. It's an old tradition, which is strong in Kerry. Whatever it is I hate to see a bird coming into a house. It gives me a bad feeling.

Yet I still think that robins are beautiful birds. They are lovely and gentle. I love to see them around and there are lots of them in Kerry. I would never harm one and I would be terribly upset if someone killed one. I would hate that. I love to see them in the trees and on the lawn but, whatever happens, just don't come in the house! It would upset me and worry me that something was to come.

MARIAN, FROM CORK, was visited by a blackbird at a time when her husband was unwell. He eventually died.

My husband passed away from a heart problem in 2001. He had been in hospital from around January until March. During all that time, while he was in hospital, there was a blackbird perched on the handle of my back door. Every single day the bird was there, sitting on the handle and looking in at me through the glass of the door.

Every time I would see him I'd say, 'My God! That bird is there again!' I remember there was snow at the time and

I thought, 'That's unusual, he's still coming.' Even when I hadn't seen him I knew he was there because he'd leave his mark on the door. I wasn't scared but it went on and on. This had never happened before.

I had got a new back door, a few months before, and it had a shiny gold handle. I initially thought it was the shine on the handle that might have been attracting the bird. But I had been telling them at work and someone said to me that the bird could be a spirit. At the time my son was ill and I was very distressed so I said, 'I'll leave the bird alone.'

My husband eventually died. After he passed away, the bird stopped coming. It was then that somebody at work said, 'Marian, when I heard you talking about the blackbird I knew there was going to be a death in your family. I didn't say anything to you earlier because I didn't want to frighten you.'

At the time my daughter was expecting and the person at work thought she was going to lose the baby. He knew a death was going to happen. He also said, 'I'll bet you the bird is gone.' He was right. The bird was gone and he was never seen anymore. Nor did a blackbird ever land on the handle again.

I said it to one of my sons, who was into reading about this sort of thing, and he said it was a pagan superstition that the blackbird was a sign of death. Someone else said that too. But I don't know what to think of it.

I had never heard of it before. But this was definitely a blackbird and there clearly was a connection. I think it was a forewarning and it certainly was most unusual that the bird sat on the handle, looking in the door.

DONNA, WHO COMES ORIGINALLY FROM COUNTY TYRONE but who now lives in County Derry, reflects on her mother's story about a bird that tapped three times on her window. She also describes visits from a robin.

My mum told me, years and years ago, that one night as she was going to bed a bird came and pecked on her window. She heard the bird tapping on the window three times. She said she knew, right away, that her granddad had died. The next day she was told he had died the previous night. But she wasn't in the least bit surprised.

My mum had been very close to her granddad. She was the blue-eyed granddaughter. They got on very well. She reckoned she had been forewarned about his death. She felt that her granddad had come to tell her. She then told me that if a bird came and it tapped on your window it was the sign that someone had died. She told me that when I was a teenager. No one else ever said it to me apart from my mother.

I don't know where my mother got the idea from. She would not really have believed in stuff like that. Her mother wouldn't have believed in things like that either. It was just that we had been talking about death when she told me. She was definitely sure there was a connection and that she was forewarned that her granddad had died.

My mum died at the age of 56. For some reason, after she had passed away, whenever I saw a robin I started thinking, 'Mummy is about.' There was no reason for it. We never discussed it. Robins weren't even something she liked. If anything I just associated robins with Christmas. But I used to see a robin sitting on the kitchen window and I would always say to my husband, 'There's that robin. Mum's here.'

For probably four or five weeks I'd always see it on the kitchen window. It was like my mum telling me, 'I'm here!' Some days I would think to myself, 'God! I'm really missing my mum.' Then, that day, the robin would appear. It always came when I was at a low ebb as if it was saying, 'Don't worry! I'm still about!'

I remember, one morning, saying to my husband, 'I haven't seen the robin in ages.' It had been on my mind. I felt a bit disheartened, a bit down in the dumps. He came down that morning and saw the robin in the kitchen. It had come in through the kitchen window. He caught it and put it out. I said, 'You should have got me up.'

About two weeks later he came upstairs and said, 'Right! Downstairs!' I said, 'What's wrong?' The robin was in the kitchen again. When I went down it was just sitting there in the kitchen, near the kitchen window. I went over and just lifted it and it didn't fly about. Out it went again.

I don't associate the robin with death in any way. It's just that after my mum died the robin appeared. If someone asked me if I thought my mum was really about I would say, 'No, she's not.' But when I miss her terribly it's great to see the robin sitting out in the back garden. I do get comfort from the robin.

Looking back at what occurred with the knocking on the window, all I can say is that it never happened to me. But I believe my mother because she was not someone to invent those sorts of stories. She probably even felt strange telling me. We didn't believe in things like that. We weren't that kind of family. But I still think about her story, now and again, and she comes into my mind every time I see a robin.

MAEVE, FROM COUNTY WEXFORD, heard knocking sounds at the time that her husband's aunt died. It happened in the late 2000s.

I was in my dining-room, one evening, about three or four years ago. The dining-room is next to the kitchen and the back door is in a porch off the kitchen. It was just after eight o'clock in the evening. I suddenly heard three knocks at the back door, like three raps on the door. There were just three knocks, one after the other. They were very clear sounds.

I knew immediately that they came from the back door. They were from that direction. They also couldn't have come from the front door because the hall is too far away. Nobody knocks on the front door, anyway, because it has a bell. Nobody comes around the back either.

I didn't do anything. I was on my own and I didn't move. I never went out to the back door because nobody comes there. I also knew it couldn't have been birds because they wouldn't have been around at eight o'clock at night. But the knocks made an impression on me as I went off to bed.

The next morning my brother-in-law rang me and said that his aunt had died that morning. I didn't know her very well, although I had met her a few times. She was my husband's aunt and wasn't very close to me. She was a lovely woman but lived a good bit away.

For some strange reason I wasn't happy with what my brother-in-law said. I thought, 'God! I heard three knocks last night!' I said, 'I'm going to question this. I'm going to check this out.' So I rang him back and asked him for his aunt's daughter's number.

I rang her even though I didn't know her that well. I asked her, 'What time did your mother die?' There was something niggling me. She said, 'She died last night, shortly after eight o'clock.' My brother-in-law had been wrong – it wasn't in the morning but it was actually the night before that she had died, just after eight o'clock. She had died at what seems to have been the exact same time that I heard the knocking. I had heard the three knocks just after eight.

I couldn't believe it. I really did get a bit of a fright. Why I had gone to the trouble of checking I just can't imagine. It was strange that I rang and questioned the time. It really doesn't matter what time a person died at. But I had the three knocks on my mind, for some reason. I must have been thinking, 'My God! I wonder did she die last night!'

I rang a friend of mine. She had someone with her. She told him my story and I started to cry with the fright because he said, 'Oh! It could be evil.' I also said to my husband, 'Why did I hear the knocks when I hardly knew her?' She had really nothing to do with me. Why me? My husband didn't even see this aunt very often.

I don't know what it was. I never heard of anything like this before. There was no tradition of it in my family. Was it a bit of a coincidence? Or maybe people come when they are dying, to let you know? I just don't know. But I still wonder, 'Why did I hear the knocks? And why did I question it? Why did I ring my brother-in-law and ask him for the number?' It certainly is odd. But that's what happened. I think about it all the time and it has always stuck in my mind.

MARIE, FROM COUNTY WEXFORD, **also heard sounds at her back door, this time on the night of her sister-in-law's 'month's mind'. The year was 1984.**

My sister-in-law had been sick for a year but had died rather quickly in the end. She was young and we were quite close. It was a very sad situation. She had lived near me and she always came down to the side of our house to come in. She never used the front door. I live in a bungalow but the back is split-level and you would have to go up a few steps to get to the door. That's the way she always came into the house.

At that time our back door had a brown Bakelite door-knob on it. It was a loose sort of doorknob and it was round. The door also had a half-glass window with a little curtain inside. But no one else came in that way because they would have to come down by the side of the house. Nobody would be in the back garden anyway.

One early August night, after my sister-in-law's 'month's mind', I was sitting with my daughter in the living-room. We had all been at the mass and it was now 11 o'clock at night. There's a big window in the living-room and you can see down the garden. The living-room is next to the kitchen. I suddenly heard the handle of the kitchen door turn one way and then turn again and again. It turned three times. I said nothing and my daughter said nothing, although she had heard it too.

I looked out the window from where I was sitting. But I didn't see anyone. I also went out to the kitchen but I didn't open the back door. I suppose I was a bit nervous in case I'd see something strange. I knew I wasn't going to see anything, anyway, because nobody would come in through the back. There was nobody there. So I went back into the living-room and my daughter and I said nothing for ages. But then she said, 'That was my aunt!' We didn't really talk about it after that.

The next morning my sister-in-law's daughter came over to our house. She had come home for the 'month's mind'. She said, 'Something strange happened this morning. I got out of bed and the room was very stuffy. I went down to get a cup of tea and then decided to go back and open up the windows and freshen up the place. But when I went back to the bedroom I got the most beautiful smell of flowers and roses.' She said to herself, 'My mother is here!'

I said to her, 'You sit down and I'll tell you what happened over here.' I told her about what had happened the night before and what I had heard and I said, 'Your mother was here last night. She was here first before she went to you.' I'd say she was quite pleased and happy about it. She was also sure her mother was in her bedroom that morning.

I am definite nobody came in the back. They would have had to come up the steps behind the window where I was and I would have seen them. My curtains weren't even drawn; they were open. And it's a big window so I could see right down the garden. There was nobody there. And nobody has ever come to the back door like that.

I think my sister-in-law definitely came back. Nothing else could have moved the doorknob. I knew the sound. I also know the type she was. She would say, 'I'll do this now and give this one a bit of a fright.' She would have fun doing it. She would be breaking her heart laughing. That's the type she was.

I am convinced that she came to my back door that night. I really believe that's what happened. And I certainly believe my sister-in-law was there. I can't think of any other logical explanation.

PATRICIA, FROM COUNTY TYRONE, **explains how glowing red lights have often been seen by her family before tragedies take place.**

My mother and father were living in England after they got married. This was back in the early 1950s. They moved across and my daddy was working there. They had no family of their own, at the time, and they were living in a wee bedsit. It was sparsely furnished. Hanging down from the ceiling was a bare bulb, as there was no lampshade. There was a big mirror on the wall.

One night they were lying in bed. My dad noticed that the light-bulb shone up bright red in the mirror, which was opposite the bed. But the bulb that was hanging from the ceiling wasn't red at all. My dad felt it was very strange. He said to my mum, 'Do you see that?' She was looking at the bulb hanging from the ceiling and she said, 'See what?' He then explained what he saw.

The next morning my mother got a telegram to say that her father in Ireland wasn't well. Daddy couldn't go home but my mum did. The following night he was getting ready for bed and he was smoking a cigarette at the side of the bed before he got in. He was sitting with his arms on his knees. Suddenly, for no good reason, his cigarette glowed bright red. He hadn't pulled on the cigarette or anything like that.

My dad wondered about the bulb, the previous night, and the news they had got. He started thinking, 'Oh, God! I hope nothing has happened back in Ireland.' My mum's dad was the first thing he thought of. He was very worried. The next morning another telegram arrived to say that my mum's dad had passed away.

My dad was convinced, from then on, that what had happened wasn't normal. He felt both cases were strange. He always found that something like a strange, bright red light forewarned him of bad things to come. He thought these red lights signalled danger and that it wasn't a good thing when you saw them.

My dad and mum eventually came home from England. One day my dad and my sister were driving in the car. It was dark. They were coming down the hill near Brougher Mountain, which is close to where we live. This was back in 1971, during the Troubles. My sister suddenly pointed out to my father what seemed like a tail-light on a bike. She had a glimpse of it ahead. She said, 'Watch out, there's a guy ahead with a tail-light.' My dad said, 'I've seen it.' He also thought it might have been a man on a bike.

When they got down the hill there was no tail-light there whatsoever. There was no man and no bike and no animal, nothing on the road. Yet both of them had seen the light and it was red. My dad felt, once again, that there was something wrong and something was going to happen. A few days later five people were killed in an explosion at Brougher Mountain.

I had a similar experience involving a bright light. It concerned my dad's brother. I came in from work, one night, and the children were up in bed. I eventually decided to go on up to bed myself. I always raked the fire before I did. I remember doing it that night, at about 12 o'clock. There was nothing left in the grate but dead ashes.

At around three o'clock my daughter woke up with an earache. I went down the stairs to get some medicine. From the top of the stairs I could see a red glow on the wall of the hall. I wondered, 'Has someone gone to bed and left the light on?' I then remembered that I was the last one up. So I went down the stairs and noticed that the bright glow was coming from the living-room.

I went into the living-room and I was shocked to see a flame about six inches high coming from a charred stick in the fire. It wasn't at all like a dying flame. It looked like it was coming from a firelighter that had just been lit. It was a big, strong flame. I just stood and looked at it and thought, 'That fire was out when I went to bed. I know it was dead. That's strange.' I went out to the kitchen and got the medicine and when I came back in the fire was just a wee flicker. I then went back upstairs.

Soon afterwards we got news that my uncle had dropped dead. His death was a shock and a surprise. I immediately thought of the bright flame. The flame was there three hours after the fire had gone dead. No one else had come downstairs. My seeing it was also followed by something bad. The whole thing was most strange. I wondered was it my dad, who had recently passed away, at that stage, giving me a sign about his brother and that he was going to drop dead.

I have had other experiences too. I remember coming home from work, one night, and I saw a red light opposite a man's house. I thought it might have been a bike but it wasn't and it puzzled me. A short time later we heard that the man was badly ill and he died soon after. It was a red light again.

I don't have any explanation for the connection between a red glow and things happening that are bad. I don't believe it's a coincidence. It's almost a case of 'red for danger'. I never get any sign for goodness and I have never come across anything giving me good news. But there is definitely a connection with the red light and it's not good when you see it.

I think there are strange things out there. If your mind is relaxed and open to things, you might experience them. And I believe in premonitions and warnings. Maybe they come from loved ones who have already passed away. I'd like to think it's from them, giving us warnings that something bad is ahead.

DAN, FROM COUNTY CORK, recalls the extraordinary way a family bereavement was anticipated. He was aged 17 at the time it occurred. Similar to the previous story, 'light' played a prominent role.

In January 1965 my mother was sitting at our kitchen table. She was in her 50s. It was during the morning. I wasn't there because I was at school. But my father, who hadn't been well, was there. One brother and a sister of mine were there as well. And, of course, my mother was there too.

The kitchen table was rectangular. My father used to sit at one side of the table and my brother used to sit just alongside him. That brother, however, wasn't there that morning because he had gone to work. My other brother and sister were at the other side of the table. My mother was sitting at the top.

My mother suddenly saw a light flashing over the table, as they were eating. The light shone just around where my father was sitting. She described it as a kind of slow form of lightning. It flashed slowly over that one part of the table. She knew it wasn't sunlight coming in or anything like that. There were no other lights there. She said it, there and then, but my father just laughed it off.

She thought it had something to do with my father because he was in bad health. He had a bad pain in his back, which eventually turned out to be osteoporosis, although that wasn't known at the time. Because of that she was sure that what she had seen had to do with him.

She got such a fright that, although they were due to go into Cork that day to do shopping, she decided they wouldn't go. It was a big event to travel into the city in those times, but she decided to cancel. She was afraid that something was going to happen and that my father was going to die in town.

It went right out of my mother's head for a few months. She never spoke about it during that time. But then, the following April, she received very bad news. One day people came into the yard to tell her that her son – my brother – had been in an accident. He was aged 21 and worked for a neighbouring farmer.

I think the people who came in said, 'He's not too bad.' But my mother immediately replied, 'I know he's finished.' That was the same brother who should have been sitting beside my father at breakfast, that morning, but had gone to work instead. I will never forget the day, as I was doing my oral Irish test at the time.

What had happened was that he was on the back of a tractor and was going from one farm to another. He was travelling along the road and something caused him to fall off the back. He crashed the rear of his head into the ground. He had other injuries as well. They could never find out why he had fallen, although they knew he had been standing up at the back of the tractor and he had probably lost his balance and fallen off. He lived for less than a day and then he died.

It was strange what had happened. Although my mother had believed the light was over my father, she then realised that it was actually over where my brother used to sit. From where she was sitting, she couldn't really tell the difference. Where they sat was only about one foot apart. It was only because my father wasn't well that she was led to believe it had to do with him.

There was another strange thing relating to it. That same brother who died had worked for a different farmer before that. One day he and another man who worked for the farmer were setting grain in a field. He suddenly saw lights inside an outhouse, as they were loading up the grain. The whole barn lit up for about ten seconds.

He said it to the man who was working with him but he said he saw nothing. That same man was killed that evening as he went home on a tractor. He was going through a crossroads where there was no right-of-way at the time. A car came and hit the back of the tractor wheel and turned the tractor upside down. The man died as a result.

There was a further event as well. My uncle had a son who died in the Congo in 1960. He was in the army and was killed at the Niemba ambush. My mother always said she had a sense about that. She always said that she didn't feel right, that day, and something was bothering her all day long. She couldn't put her finger on it. She eventually heard on the radio that Irish soldiers had been killed in the Congo and she knew it had to do with that. It turned out that my first cousin had been killed.

I remember that same uncle came down to visit us one day.

He used to visit us regularly. But this day, in the course of the conversation, my uncle, who was very religious, wondered aloud about life after death. My mother responded, 'There's something there alright!' She was referring to what had happened with my brother and the light.

My mother was a very religious person. She would do the First Fridays and the Rosary and all that sort of thing. I think she associated what happened with her religious beliefs. And anytime anybody would mention something afterwards about what had happened, she would say, 'I know there's something there!' She wouldn't elaborate but she would use what happened with my brother as a yardstick.

I would be a bit of a sceptic myself. If I was told a story like that, and it came from somebody else, I probably wouldn't believe it. But I know this to be true. Why would my mother invent it? There was no reason for her to make it up. She also described, at the time, what she saw.

I have often heard stories like it, involving certain families having premonitions before deaths. I have, however, buried my mother and my father and two brothers and I've never seen anything myself. I couldn't say I encountered any premonitions or anything else. But I'm still convinced of what happened with my mother. For the rest of her life she said that she knew something was going to happen and I believe she was telling the truth.

PATRICIA, WHO COMES ORIGINALLY FROM DUBLIN, tells the story of how she came into possession of a ring. This final narrative involves the death of a friend and neighbour.

I was looking after this old couple, who I got to know. They were poor. They had no family whatsoever and no one to look after them. They once said to me, 'It costs a lot for us to go by taxi to the hospital.' I said, 'For goodness sake! Any day you are going, give me a shout and I will take you there.' I did that over the years.

My husband would look after them as well. We used to visit them and bring them presents at Christmas because they had nothing. The woman started referring to me as her sister. Everywhere we went she would introduce me by saying, 'This is my sister.' People used to look at me because she was an old woman and I wasn't.

One Christmas she gave me a present of some perfume out of the chemist's. She gave me a small box as well and said, 'I want you to have this because you are the closest person to me in my life. It's my engagement ring.' I said, 'Absolutely no way! I'm not taking it. You have a niece in England and you should give it to her. It's right that she should have it.' So she took the ring back.

Sometime later the woman became unwell and went into hospital. She was getting a cataract done. I told her not to get it done because she suffered from blood pressure. I said, 'Don't get it done until I can be with you, in case anything goes wrong.' But she went ahead and got it done anyway. The medical records in the hospital show that when she went in she put me down as her sister under her next of kin.

The next day she had a stroke. I went up to the hospital a few times to see her. They then called me, one night, and said, 'You had better come quickly. She is after taking another stroke.' So I dashed to the hospital but she had died five minutes before I arrived. I actually arrived at four o'clock and she had died five minutes earlier.

Eleven weeks later her husband died. He had been heart-broken, literally. The woman's brother came home from England and went through her house and took whatever he wanted including a box of jewellery and bankbooks. He then went away.

A day or so later, before the funeral, he rang and asked me if I could go into the house and get a few more things including her birth cert. He needed them. I said I would but I decided to get a Guard to come with me.

The Guard and I went in and got what we were asked to get. The Guard then said, 'Is there anything else you need to look for?' I said, 'No, not really.' He said, 'You know, old people can leave money in houses.' I said, 'They had nothing.' We looked around the house anyway and came across an old wardrobe upstairs. It was locked. He said, 'With your permission I'll open it.' So I said, 'Go ahead. That's fine.'

Quick as a flash he had the wardrobe open. There was a handbag in there. He gave it to me and said, 'You should go through that. I don't have the authority.' So I went through it and found some money. But I also found the engagement ring.

When I saw it I thought, 'Oh, my goodness! That was the ring she was going to give me last Christmas.' It was still in the box. The Guard took the money into custody. I kept the bag and ring with me and that night I gave them both to her brother.

When I gave them to him he immediately looked at the ring. He closed the box again and gave it back to me. He said, 'You know something. I have a feeling that my sister would have loved you to have that. After all you did for her I feel she would like you to have it.' I was taken aback. I was amazed. I couldn't believe what he was just after saying.

So he gave me the ring back. I said, 'It's not my place to have that ring. You have a daughter and you should give it to her.' But he said again, 'I have a feeling she would want you to have it.' And he added, 'You were like a sister to her.' It was most strange. He couldn't have known that she had wanted me to have the ring or that she had called me her sister.

The next day his wife said, 'I heard how you were given the

engagement ring. I'm so happy because I know she never wore the ring and she'd be only too pleased for you to have it. You were like a sister to her.' I thought that was unbelievable too. She couldn't have known it either. I had never told them. I had never said anything about her referring to me as her sister. I had never even met them before in my life.

What happened was way beyond coincidence. It was strange that the Guard had said, 'Do you want to check anywhere else?' There was nothing else of value in the house. Her jewellery box was already taken away. There was no reason for us to look inside the wardrobe. That wardrobe would have been thrown out with all the other rubbish and no one would have ever gone through it. But I was drawn to the wardrobe and eventually I got the ring back.

What happened was certainly most unusual. Through the strangest of ways, I ended up owning the ring. When I was with the Guard it was like she had said to me, 'Go to the wardrobe!' I still have her ring now and I wear it all the time. It's gorgeous. It means so much to me. I absolutely love it and I love wearing it. And I always feel its owner is smiling down at me all the time because she wanted me to have it.

THE BURDEN OF PROOF

Throughout 1996 and early 1997 a most extraordinary research experiment was conducted at the University of Nevada with the aim of establishing whether humans can see into the future. The basic tools of the experiment were simple – a straight-backed chair, a computer, some coloured pictures, a few complicated machines sprouting various paraphernalia and a selection of volunteers drawn from staff, faculty and students.

The instigator of the experiment was the hugely innovative psychologist and scientist Dr. Dean Radin. His basic premise was simple. If people can see into the future, he reasoned, then they are likely to become agitated and aroused when they see something ahead that is disturbing and negative. On the other hand, they are likely to become calm and serene when they see something that is tranquil and peaceful.

A panel of volunteers was chosen for the experiment. Each, in turn, was placed in front of a computer screen and once seated was hooked up to sensors measuring heart rate and sweating, among other indicators of arousal. Two different sets of images were inserted in the computer – emotional images such as erotic and violent scenes, and calm images such as landscapes and portraits.

Each volunteer was then requested to place his hand on a computer mouse. Once the mouse was clicked, the computer screen stayed blank for five seconds. Immediately the five seconds had elapsed, however, either an emotional image or a calm image – randomly selected by the computer – showed up on the screen.

As we might expect, indicators revealed that during the five seconds before the image appeared the volunteers showed increased arousal levels. That was no surprise. After all, they were anticipating something that was about to occur, whatever that might be. Excitement was mounting. That was exactly what the research team expected.

Remarkably, however, the level of arousal *increased by an even greater amount* before an emotional picture showed than before a calm image showed. In other words, during the five second wait the volunteers were anticipating the precise sort of image that was about to appear. What's more, they were anticipating the type of image even before the computer had randomly selected it. The volunteers, quite simply, were predicting the future!

Radin used some 24 volunteers in his research study, testing outcomes over and over again. Following three similar studies conducted soon after, the combined results showed a distinct – and statistically significant – pattern. The overall conclusion was stunning – the odds of the combined outcomes happening by chance, and not being a genuine presentiment effect, were a remarkable 125,000 to one against.

To put it mildly, Radin's conclusions raised some serious issues for the physical sciences. Most importantly, his results questioned the scientific concept of time, which holds that we emerge from past time, live in present time but cannot foresee an unknowable future. Additionally, they forced us to reassess our understanding of premonitions and precognition.

The experiments also baffled and impressed Nobel Prize winner Dr. Kary Mullis. Dr. Mullis, incidentally, discovered how to mass duplicate DNA, one of the greatest inventions of the twentieth century. 'I could see about three seconds into the future,' Mullis remarked, having paid a visit to Radin and participated in a demonstration trial. 'There's something funny about time that we don't understand because you shouldn't be able to do that.'

Not content with showing that we can see into the future, Dr. Radin initiated another experiment to establish if 'gut feelings' were real. It was not an easy task. How do you check if 'butterflies in the tummy' or 'gut-wrenching sensations' have genuine meaning? How do you assess the general bodily uneasiness or feelings of apprehension that so often warn us of trouble ahead? How do you examine the sinking feelings that frequently precede news of a death from afar?

It was precisely this challenge that Radin set out to tackle. To begin with, a volunteer – referred to as a 'receiver' – was selected and placed in a room. The volunteer was attached to what is called an electrogastrogram, which senses and records the electrical current generated by movements of the stomach muscles. When a person experiences emotional sensations, a clenching of the gut is revealed. When sensations are neutral, there is a calm response.

Another volunteer – referred to as a 'sender' – was placed in a nearby room. Sequences of emotional images or neutral images were then shown to this second volunteer. The volunteer was asked, once a sequence was shown, to focus on his fellow volunteer – the 'receiver' – and to try to mentally send the emotions he felt. A check was then made of the recordings taken by the electrogastrogram.

The results were astonishing. They showed that electrical responses in the gut were significantly higher when emotional sensations, as opposed to neutral sensations, were sent. The gut literally tightened more, or clenched more, when these sensations were transmitted. Radin concluded: 'It may turn out that the belly brain's intuition is more connected with the rest of the world, and with other people, than previously suspected.'

Important though his conclusions were, Radin's remit in his experiments was to assess whether we could see or feel the future but not to establish the reasons why. 'The problem is that we don't really know how to explain it,' Radin later remarked of his overall observation that we can perceive or sense what's ahead, 'and because of that people get very uncomfortable and say, "Well, it might not be real." But I think that's just nonsense.' It is to this strange territory – examining the reasons why – that we now turn our attention.

Let's start with a fascinating proposition which claims that the brain records and stores events only to replay them at a later stage. This theory sounds complicated but it isn't. It proposes that there is a time lapse between happenings being recorded by the brain and, on the other hand, the time they surface in our consciousness. Should this premise be true, then all conscious events which we perceive as occurring in the present are only old events that are now coming to our attention.

The process can be compared to the use of a DVD recorder. Acting in exactly the same way as the brain, we might record a TV programme on a DVD. Having completed the process, we don't view the programme and we don't know what it's about until later, when we sit down and watch it. The brain, in an identical way, records the events of our life but it is only later on that it brings them to our conscious attention.

It follows, therefore, that if we could get a sneak preview of the DVD of our lives we might spot things ahead. Perhaps, occasionally, there's some sort of jump on the tape, allowing us this kind of snap view of the future. Proponents argue that it might be during these jumps in the tape that we experience forewarnings.

Alternatively, there may be unusual brain configurations or abnormalities or even chemical imbalances that allow certain people to tap into the recordings. Although the research behind this theory is far from conclusive, it is groundbreaking nevertheless and may help us explain much of what we have been talking about in this book.

It should also be noted that this theory has implications way beyond identifying the mechanism that gives us future sight. If what you are doing right now, as you read this, is an activity which happened some time ago but is only now emerging into your consciousness then a worrying question must be asked. The question is this – what is the extent of the time lapse, a millisecond maybe, or could it be longer, maybe even 100 years? Perhaps, some argue, we might already be dead but we just haven't come to that part of the recording yet!

A further theory proposes that consciousness may be universal and that our premonitions and dreams are drawn from this vast cosmic ocean spanning space and time. Universal consciousness may embrace not only all space but all time including the past, present and future. Our own consciousness, some scientists argue, may not be located in, or specific to, our brains. Instead, our bodies may be more like antennae tapping into this boundless infinity.

Should this be so, our ability to pluck insights from this immense cosmic reality may explain how we can occasionally see ahead. As the famous nineteenth-century scholar and mind researcher Frederic Myers put it, sometimes this scheme is 'liable to leakages and to occasional rupture,' thus allowing us to identify what lies before us. We may, in this way, occasionally sense or perceive future events.

Another closely-associated theory was put forward by the extraordinary Irishman John William Dunne, who was born in County Kildare back in 1875. Dunne was, quite literally, a 'dreamer'. He dreamt, with uncanny accuracy, of the violent eruption of Mount Pelée, Martinique, in 1902. He dreamt of a tragic factory fire in Paris. He once even dreamt that his watch had stopped at a particular time only to discover on awakening that indeed it had.

Intrigued by these strange forewarnings, Dunne turned his attention to explaining them. The answer, he concluded, lies in the nature of time. Peculiarly, he noted, some of his dreams reviewed events from the past while others foresaw events from the future. How could it be, he wondered, that our minds seem to flit across the past and the future while in a dreaming state but only focus on the present while we are awake?

The reason, Dunne postulated, is that all time is eternally present, with the past, present and future happening together and part of a unified reality. It is only in sleep, however, that the mind wanders freely. Only then can we drift through the past, present and future with carefree abandon. When we are awake, in sharp contrast, the mind interprets time in a linear, one-directional fashion.

Dunne suggested that we can best understand what occurs by imagining we are playing a piano. In the awakened state we play the piano keys one after another in sequence, from left to right. Our hand travels in only one direction, note after note. By way of contrast, while asleep we become virtuosos, flashing to and fro across the keyboard, moving all over the piano and interpreting the full span of keys at will.

Lest we dismiss Dunne as some sort of quaint eccentric, espousing outlandish and laughable views, it is worth noting that he became one of the most highly-respected thinkers of his time. Not only was he an aeronautical engineer and inventor of international renown but his work on dreams and his theories on time were well-received. Authors J. B. Priestley and Aldous Huxley ranked among his admirers. He died in 1949.

Although seemingly outlandish a century ago, it is worth noting that Dunne's theories have gained renewed credence with recent developments in the magical world of quantum physics. This is a world of complicated theories that challenge our long-held views of reality. It is a strange world where matter can move from one spot to another without travelling through the intervening space, where information can move instantly over vast distances.

It is a place of worlds within worlds, of parallel universes, of multiple realities, of infinite consciousness, where future events already exist and where premonitions and precognition may merely represent the brain's retrieval of memories from the life we have yet to experience. It is, however, a complex sphere of mathematical formulae and subatomic particles that lies outside the remit of this chapter.

Let's move instead to the possible involvement of another phenomenon and its potential links to foreseeing the future. The phenomenon in question is telepathy. The word comes from the Greek *tēle* meaning 'distant' and *pathos* meaning 'feeling' and involves the transference of thoughts or ideas from one person to another in ways other than by using the five senses.

The concept of telepathy dates back to the late nineteenth century and was an early target for investigation by the Society for Psychical Research, which in 1886 published its findings regarding telepathy in the famous work *Phantasms Of The Living*. From an early stage, its potential role in explaining both premonitions and precognition has also been examined.

The possible involvement of telepathy can be very simply

explained. For example, a person may receive a telepathic communication from another person whose health is badly failing. The recipient then constructs a mental image of the other person lying on their deathbed. He tells family and friends about his 'premonition' of the other person's death, which duly happens.

Major accidents may be foreseen in an identical way. A railway engineer may be deeply concerned about the state of the points on the tracks to the extent that he believes an accident is inevitable. He may be so concerned that he passes this information telepathically to others. The recipients then conceptualise a train disaster occurring as a result of failed points. Once again, the apparent forewarning is seen as a 'premonition' of the subsequent tragedy.

The eminent parapsychologist Professor Ian Stevenson, from the University of Virginia, was attracted to this theory and explains it well. 'It is possible,' he concluded, 'that the subject, by paranormal means, gains access to information from which, once it is available to him, he can infer the future course of events. The sum of his inferences is then projected in the form of visual or other images which he relates to the future.'

Stevenson, however, accepted that the telepathy hypothesis fails to explain forewarnings that identify events from years ahead which subsequently come true. He also accepted that the hypothesis is inadequate at explaining the positive results that arise in some experiments where genuinely strict random techniques are used. It is, in other words, an incomplete explanation, according to Stevenson.

So far, I have ignored another important factor and its possible role in explaining at least some cases of foresight or future perception. The factor in question is intuition. Although mentioned in chapter one, let's remind ourselves once again what it is. Defining it simply, it is that ability we all seem to have which allows us to know or comprehend things without being aware of where the knowledge or insight originates.

Coming from deep down inside, intuition defies rational explanation and is our body's sixth sense. It enables us to assess events and it helps steer us in the wisest and most advantageous direction. We often use it to advise us of the very best course of action to take. It can also arm us with seemingly inexplicable insights to the future.

Intuition can be readily explained. Although seldom aware of doing it, we constantly scan our horizon for information. When we walk down the street, we hear many sounds – some of them non-threatening, others ominous and menacing; some emanating from close by, others from a distance. We take in the noise of traffic. We interpret sounds of people – some engaged in innocent chatter, others showing signs of violence or aggression. Vast amounts of extraneous noises are digested subconsciously.

We also sense energy – those vibrations and feelings that have driven all cosmic events since the Big Bang and the emergence of man. We can sense vibrant, resonant, sonorous energy, with all its positive connotations of happiness and good health. We can also sense energy decay. We can even sense the finer, more delicate vibrations of thought and emotion and the implications they have for life to come.

Our full range of senses, including sight, sound, taste, smell and touch, are all on constant alert, probing, scanning, retrieving, sorting, storing and analysing information while providing us with insights to the future. We are, in effect, like some sort of complex, sponge-like computer, soaking up all this external intelligence which our subconscious assimilates and digests. This store of knowledge, stockpiled deep inside, warns us of what may lie ahead.

We may, perhaps, meet a relative or an acquaintance on the

street. A sudden, indefinable feeling might overcome us that we will never again see that person alive. The feeling cannot be accounted for, rationalised or explained. The sensation is strange, defying logic or reason. It may well be like a flash of perception. Possibly, however, it may be derived from our intuitive senses assessing and evaluating body language, voice inflexion, facial expressions or physical appearance. An uncommon choice of words may have been noticed. Unusual energy patterns may have been detected.

This wonderful power emerges from our mind's deep subterranean recesses where our emotions and memories are stored. It is from there that our intuitive perception comes, not from our conscious mind where our capacity for logic and reason is located. What's more, studies definitively show that whenever there is a conflict between the two – the conscious and the subconscious mind – the winner is always the subconscious.

That this is so is impressively illustrated in a fascinating investigation undertaken at the University of Iowa under the guidance of researcher Dr. Antoine Bechara. This landmark study examined the respective roles of conscious and nonconscious factors in gamblers' decision-making. Its ultimate achievement was to highlight the strange and powerful role of our subconscious senses when assessing the future ahead.

The Bechara experiment was most ingenious. Volunteers were asked to select cards, one by one, from different decks. They were told that each time they selected a card they would win some money. The aim was to maximise the amount they won. What they weren't told, however, was that some of the decks were loaded. The bad decks contained a higher percentage of losing cards; the good decks contained a higher proportion of winning cards.

At ten-card intervals, the volunteers were each asked simple questions to ascertain how they felt the game was going. The questions were straightforward – 'tell me all you know about what is going on in this game' and 'tell me how you feel about this game.' Their responses would indicate if they were becoming conscious of the bias inherent in the packs.

Inevitably, after some time, the volunteers caught on to the fact that the game and the decks were rigged. At a particular point, it became clear from their answers and from the way they gradually gravitated to the good decks that they had developed a hunch. Later on, from their answers and from the way they chose more and more cards from the good decks, it was obvious that they had the game figured out.

What I have neglected to mention, though, was that the volunteers had also been linked up to polygraphs to measure the activity of the sweat glands under the skin in the hands. How these sweat glands behave tells us about the unconscious, involuntary actions of the nervous system. When stress or anxiety levels rise, the sweat glands become more active. When levels fall, their activity diminishes.

Remarkably, the polygraph results showed that, as bad cards from bad decks were chosen, volunteers' stress levels rose long before they consciously knew what was going on. The levels were increasing well ahead of when the volunteers began to voice any concern about the loaded decks. In other words, the subconscious was advising volunteers what choices to make *before* they had any conscious recognition that the game was rigged, proving – for those of us who didn't already suspect it – that our subconscious is light years ahead of our conscious in figuring out the future ahead.

For some people, however, all of these discussions about intuition, premonitions, precognition and 'seeing the future' are nonsense and the truth they say is far more mundane – namely, that all of these phenomena are merely fortuitous happenings that occur by chance. A forewarned-of outcome, they argue, is no more than an accidental result, determined by luck or coincidence and subject to the laws of probability.

Undoubtedly, some forewarnings fall into this bracket. For example, a person may dream of a plane crash only to find that one occurs on a faraway continent the following day. It is reasonable to propose that, given the general prevalence of dreams involving plane crashes and the number of crashes that occur in a year, the connection between these two events – the dream and the crash – might be spurious.

The 'law of large numbers' warns us that something along these same lines will happen occasionally, by chance. All of us have many dreams each night and a number of them will sometimes involve plane crashes. With the world's population at seven billion, that's a lot of dreams. Likewise, although plane crashes are rare, many do occur, including large and small collisions and those involving passenger aircraft and freight craft as well. There could well be a huge number of people dreaming of plummeting planes on any night preceding a crash!

Sceptics also argue that after an event, such as a crash or a death, we may rationalise that we saw it coming. Perhaps we have some sort of need to believe that we knew it would happen. That need may lead us to read too much into chance remarks or occurrences, viewed retrospectively. Indeed, after an event we may selectively recall particular images from the numerous fanciful ideas that we generate daily about happenings that might occur ahead. While doing so, perhaps thousands of other images are conveniently forgotten.

It is also possible that we sometimes mistake predictions which are based on information or experience for premonitions or precognition. For example, we may have a 'premonition' that it will rain on our forthcoming wedding date. The fact that the wedding date is set for February ensures that, given weather patterns, there is a good probability that it will. We may likewise interpret as a forewarning that we will bump into someone in a particular place, on a particular day. The fact that perhaps we work in close proximity to the other person may be conveniently overlooked. These are not 'premonitions'.

Another theory proposes that, at least in some cases, we may unwittingly bring about the future events we foresee. In other words, having anticipated that something will happen, we then set out to ensure that it does. An extreme version of this syndrome is portrayed in the film *The Medusa Touch*, where the actor Richard Burton plays a novelist who can psychically trigger major catastrophes including an air crash. On a more mundane level, it is easy to see how an ordinary person who foresees himself collapsing in the street might actually bring this about through sheer willpower.

This possibility – that we can 'will' future events to occur – has been studied under experimental conditions. One of the first of these investigations was initiated back in the 1930s by American Dr. Joseph Banks Rhine, who is widely considered to be the father of modern parapsychology. He conducted a long series of tests involving gambling and, more specifically, the throwing of dice.

Rhine's interest in gambling was prompted by the arrival at his Duke University laboratory of a gambler who claimed to be able to 'will' dice to do as he wished. Rhine began a series of tests. If the results showed that the gambler could influence outcomes then it might indicate that we, as human beings, can also influence future events. Our forewarnings, therefore, might come true because, once we conceptualise them, we can wish or will them to occur.

In the first of these tests, the gambler threw the dice by hand. Fearful that special tricks might be used to influence the throwing process, Rhine then insisted that the dice were thrown from special cups. Later on, he used machines. In all cases, the gambler was asked not to *predict* the fall of the dice but to influence the outcome by *wishing* or *willing* it to occur.

By the end of 1941, after a total of more than 650,000 dice throws, the overall experiment was declared a sustained and consistent, although controversial, success. The combined outcome of the various tests had stunning odds – 10,115 to one against – of being due only to chance. The result indicated a significant role for the power of mind over matter and that our ability to will things to happen can have a role to play in affecting the fall of dice.

A further highly-amusing yet interesting trial arose as a result of Dr. J. B. Rhine's initial gambling experiments. The establishment of this intriguing sideshow was prompted by a divinity student named William Gatling, who believed that Rhine's basic premise was not only misleading but downright wrong. The power to influence events, he argued, has nothing to do with gamblers 'willing' them to happen. Instead, it is a God-given power which is best exercised through prayer!

The stage was set for a battle of the moral extremes. The four best crapshooters on the Duke campus were selected. Four divinity students also stepped forward. The ringmaster was J. B. Rhine. 'History does not record the atmosphere or the intensity with which each side worked. Only the mathematical outcome is on record,' wrote Dr. Louisa Rhine, Rhine's wife. 'But presumably the young divinity students were just as determined to beat the crapshooters as the latter were not to be outdone by fledgling preachers.'

The outcome was fascinating – both sides won, although the two sets of scores were so similar to one another that neither the gamblers nor the divinity students could be declared the outright winner. However, both teams – separately and together – beat chance in the outcomes they achieved while rolling the dice. It was estimated that the odds of their combined score being down to chance were in excess of one million to one against – an extraordinary victory for both God and man and an indication that both could influence future events!

Without a doubt, all of the above factors, at one stage or another, might explain at least some so-called 'premonitions'. The big question remains, though, as to why – when the forewarnings appear to be genuine and real – it is mostly negative experiences, including tragedies, accidents or deaths, and not pleasant experiences that are usually foreseen. Why are the future events normally of a dark, dramatic intensity and not of a light or frivolous nature? How come so few of the events concern issues such as job promotions, life achievements or matters of value and worth.

The answer, it would seem, is contained in the question itself – namely, it may be the intensity of the event that helps determine whether or not it is sensed. By intensity is meant the amount of force, power or energy that is present. The extent of volatility and changeability may be relevant too. It's worth noting that dark events generally have the greatest intensity.

Some interesting work on this issue was undertaken by the well-known consciousness researcher Stephan A. Schwartz. He established a series of 'remote viewing' trials examining the apparent ability that people have to gather information about a distant or unseen target by sensing that target in the mind. While focusing on an image contained in a photograph, volunteers were asked by Schwartz to come up with as much information about that image as they could manage.

Although the investigation involved numerous pictures, and also consisted of many hundreds of sessions, one image that repeatedly seemed easiest for volunteers to describe was a photograph of USS Enterprise, the world's first nuclear-powered aircraft carrier. It was, by far, the most accurately identified. Although the volunteers were unaware that the carrier was nuclear powered, they regularly focused on the energy that made the vessel special, commenting that 'something very hot and fierce' or something 'like a sun inside a metal box' was associated with the ship.

The only other target selected by Schwartz that produced similar results was a solar generating station in Arizona – suggesting, once more, that intense energy, or perhaps intense energy in flux, was implicated in how volunteers responded. Schwartz concluded regarding the volunteers: 'They are particularly good at describing targets when some kind of energetic change is taking place.' Interestingly, his results were supported by further work undertaken by the nuclear physicist Edwin C. May, involving remote viewing of rocket launches and other weapons systems where, once more, massive changes of energy were involved.

We might infer, then, that it is dark events involving intense energy or dramatic changes in energy that are normally foreseen. Such events might include relatives being killed in car crashes, sons dying in war, children being stabbed on the street, daughters dying in childbirth or tragedies including the sinking of the *Titanic* and 9/11. These momentous happenings are, by their nature, 'high energy' and 'in a state of flux'. They are also precisely the sort of black, negative images that often surface in dreams.

Why, and how, these dark images break through to our consciousness is a matter of conjecture. It is reasonable to speculate, however, that intense images have a greater chance of forcing themselves through. Perhaps more benign images are also present but are too weak and feeble – indeed too lacking in energy – to make themselves felt. Instead, it is the explosive, powerful, forceful, vigorous and aggressive images that prevail.

Before concluding, it is worth examining the likelihood, or otherwise, that people who experience presentiments might somehow be able to intervene and change the events they foresee. By definition, this seems absurd. If they could do so, one might argue, it clearly wouldn't be a future event since such an event must inevitably happen.

This is not just a matter of verbal gymnastics. It might indeed be said that if people claim to have changed the direction of something in the future then what they saw certainly wasn't what lay ahead. However, it might instead be argued that the future event that was perceived wasn't a complete one and only came to full consummation once the intervention took place.

In reality, it would appear in most cases that people, having been forewarned of an event, make no attempt to alter what they have foreseen. Some, it would seem, are so unsure and uncertain that they don't intervene. Others are fearful of being ridiculed if they own up to what they saw. More are paralysed by some sort of conscious or subconscious acceptance that the future cannot be changed and to try to do so would be an exercise in folly.

The conclusions of one particular investigation bear these observations out. It was undertaken by the Rhine Research Center, based in North Carolina, which has been investigating the science of parapsychology for more than 70 years. The study in question examined 433 cases of 'future sight'. Each case contained enough threat of danger to warrant action being taken. However, in two out of three cases the individual took no steps whatsoever. For whatever reasons, these people chose not to act on what they had foreseen.

The remaining one-third of cases was different. In one out of three of these cases, people made some attempt to intervene but their efforts ended in failure. We can visualise how such a situation might arise. A person, for example, might foresee a traffic accident involving a child occurring at a particular location. Although the person stands and waits all day, in the hope of intervening, the child might suddenly appear from a gateway and rush onto the road. Instead of fate being altered, the child is killed.

But what about those remaining people whose interventions influenced future outcomes? The number is worth noting – two people in every nine. Clearly, these individuals had enough belief or determination, or maybe even desperation, to try to effect change following the events they foresaw. The fact that they succeeded proved that their initiatives were worthwhile.

That this sort of positive intervention is indeed possible is evidenced in a true-life story featured in the book *Man And Time*, written by the novelist and playwright J. B. Pricstley, who died at the age of 89 in 1984. In his book, which was published 20 years before his death, Priestley explored various theories concerning time and analysed the phenomenon of foresight. Among the stories he featured was one sent to him by an Irish woman who responded to an appeal he made while being interviewed on the BBC in 1963.

The woman described how, in a dream, she saw herself killing a three-year-old child while driving her car. The little girl, who had dark curly hair and wore a bright blue cardigan, appeared as if out of nowhere. 'On getting out, I was told that she was dead,' the woman wrote. She was understandably distressed – 'shattered' was how she put it – by how she was unable to save the girl from her inevitable fate. 'I must stress that feeling I had of inevitability,' she stated.

The morning after the dream the woman set out to visit her

daughter. She was understandably alert while driving on the same road she saw while asleep. Approaching the spot where the tragedy unfolded, she noticed that there wasn't a child in sight. Satisfied that all was well, she glanced down at her speedometer but, on looking back up, was horrified to see the exact same child of her dream standing in the middle of the road. 'I slowly brought the car to a halt, just beside her,' the relieved woman recalled.

After safely passing by, the woman continued on to her destination. Immediately upon arrival, her daughter emerged from her home, looking worried and upset. 'Why are you so worried, as I have been driving for over 30 years?' the woman asked on exiting her car. 'Oh, I know that,' the daughter responded, 'but you see, last night I had a terribly vivid dream. In this dream you ran over and killed a lovely little girl dressed in a bright blue cardigan and with lovely dark curly hair!'

It's a strange but intriguing story. It is also the ultimate paradox concerning premonitions – if our future is solidly fixed, then it cannot be changed; yet it can be seen, and because it can be seen it can be changed. 'What is this future that is sufficiently established to be observed and perhaps experienced, and yet allows itself to be altered?' a perplexed J. B. Priestley asked. That, we must conclude, is the ultimate million-dollar question concerning the forewarnings that many of us so often sense and see.

ACKNOWLEDGEMENTS

This book would not have been possible without the help of so many people who were willing to talk about their premonitions, dreams and other presentiments. Their stories dominate the bulk of the pages you have just read. Although occasionally faced with public scepticism, they agreed to disclose the intimate details of their forewarnings in the hope of informing others. Their generosity is much appreciated.

There are two excellent books I would like to recommend. Both are inspirational. The first is Dr. Larry Dossey's *The Power Of Premonitions*, which is comprehensive and easy to read. The second – Dr. Keith Hearne's *Visions Of The Future* – was first published in 1989 and, as a result, is out of print and difficult to find. This latter work, however, can often be sourced through internet sites such as Amazon or Alibris.

Few researchers in this area deserve more credit than the indefatigable Dr. Dean Radin. He is author or co-author of more than 200 technical and popular articles, a dozen book chapters and the bestselling books *Entangled Minds* and *The Conscious Universe*. His technical articles have appeared in numerous journals. Some of his studies are referred to or are available on the internet and are worth locating.

Other useful sources include *Is There An Afterlife?* by Professor David Fontana, *Beyond The Threshold* by Dr. Christopher Moreman, *Foundations Of Parapsychology* by Hoyt L. Edge et al. and *An Introduction To Parapsychology* by Dr. Harvey J. Irwin and Dr. Caroline A. Watt. Regarding dreams I would recommend *Dreams And Premonitions* by Vikas Khatri. Also valuable is Harper's classic *Encyclopedia Of Mystical And Paranormal Experience* by Rosemary Ellen Guiley.

Anyone looking for a really challenging read on the latest scientific evidence would be well advised to tackle Anthony Peake's brilliant book *Is There Life After Death?* Be warned, though, it is tough going. An older although fascinating study is John William Dunne's *An Experiment With Time*, which was published in 1927. Also of interest is Warren Weaver's *Lady Luck: The Theory Of Probability*, which covers the theme of mathematical probability and the law of averages, among other topics, in a non-technical way.

For an exemplary analysis of psychic phenomena observed during wartime, you need look no further than Hereward Carrington's stunning *Psychical Phenomena And The War*, which was published back in 1918. Paul H. Smith's *Reading The Enemy's Mind* provides a comprehensive insight to the Stargate project referred to earlier in this book.

Evan S. Connell's excellent *Son Of The Morning Star* captures the fortunes, both good and bad, of Chief Sitting Bull and General Custer at the time of the Battle of the Little Bighorn.

On the autobiographical front, Micheál Mac Liammóir's *All For Hecuba* was most helpful, as were the memoirs of psychiatrist Carl Jung, *Memories, Dreams, Reflections*, and the autobiography of author Mark Twain.

Shirley MacLaine's premonition of Peter Sellers' death is recorded in many periodicals, most notably *Weekly World News* in January 1981. Molly Allgood's experiences relating to John Millington Synge are detailed in E. H. Mikhail's *The Abbey Theatre: Interviews And Recollections*.

ACKNOWLEDGEMENTS

Bonnie McEneaney has written a thoroughly engaging book *Messages: Signs, Visits, And Premonitions From Loved Ones Lost On 9/11*, which concerns the death of her husband and other stories surrounding the devastating terrorist attacks in 2001. You will find further fascinating 9/11 narratives in a raft of other works or on the internet, notably in the Boundary Institute's site. The story of the explosion in Beatrice, Nebraska is recorded in many places but originally surfaced in *Life* magazine's edition of 27 March, 1950.

Regarding the ill-fated *Titanic* there are numerous useful sources including fashion designer and *Titanic* passenger Lady Duff Gordon's *Discretions And Indiscretions*. Also helpful were John Nolan's account of Irish survivor Patrick O'Keefe entitled *In Search Of Great Uncle Pat: Titanic Survivor* and Robin Gardiner and Dan Van Der Vat's *The Riddle Of The Titanic*.

A number of individuals have also been of assistance and are deserving of mention. Among them are Linda Monahan of Typeform, who designed the cover, and Pat Conneely, also of Typeform, who laid out the text. I am likewise grateful to Helen Keane, who provided practical help, as did Colum Kenny.

Kathleen O'Connor and Jonathan Sheils, who both read large segments of the text and advised on the cover, deserve special praise. Their comments and insights were gratefully received.

My appreciation also goes to Janet Kingston and Stephen Ryan from Limerick, and Cree and Brian Fitzgerald from Youghal, for arranging events which introduced me to a wide range of people with fascinating stories to tell.

Above all I am indebted to Úna O'Hagan for her help with this project. She advised on all stages of the work, from initial research and compilation right through to layout and design.

Úna also assisted with the unenviable task of proofing the text. Despite the theme of the book – being 'forewarned' – she could be forgiven for not anticipating the scale or the complexity of the work involved. I can't thank her enough for staying the pace.